THE PROPHET LIKE MOSES

The Evidence that Jesus was Prophesied in Deuteronomy 18:15-19

By
JAMES D. BALES

Charleston, AR:
COBB PUBLISHING
2024

Religion / Christianity / Theology / Christology
Religion / Christianity / Old Testament / Prophecy
Religion / Christianity / Prophecy / Old Testament
Religion / Christianity / Old Testament / Moses

Published in the United States of America by
Cobb Publishing
Editor@CobbPublishing.com
www.CobbPublishing.com
479.747.8372

ISBN: 978-1-960858-14-6

Introduction

Multitudes today live in a sea of uncertainty. They view nothing as authoritative and, therefore, there is nothing on which a person can depend or to which he ought to submit. They feel alienated from God, from others, and from themselves. To them, both duty and destiny are voids. In contrast with such an outlook, Christians maintain that God is, that God has spoken, that man ought to submit to the will of God, that fulfillment comes through service to God and to humanity, and that vital issues are at stake in life.

In the midst of confusion and uncertainty, Christians need to set forth the case for Christianity. Although there are many lines of evidence which constitute the case for Christianity, one aspect of this case is found in prophecy and its fulfillment. Among the prophecies there is one in which Moses, the great lawgiver of Israel, prophesied that at some time in the future he would be replaced by a prophet like unto him. Christians believe that this prophet is Jesus Christ. If this is true, certainty and meaning can be found for life. The reader is invited to think along with the author as he examines this prophecy and its fulfillment in Christ.

In some cases we have quoted from authors who lived in a century other than ours. However, scholarship was not born in our day. Furthermore, we have often referred to similar statements in modern authors, some of whom reject Christ.

Table of Contents

CHAPTER 1

The Prophecy and the Claim

In a book treasured by Jews, Moses the great prophet of Israel recorded both a promise and a warning to Israel. "God," he said, "will raise up unto thee a prophet from the midst of thee, of thy brethren, like unto me; unto him ye shall hearken; according to all that thou desired of Jehovah thy God in Horeb in the day of the assembly, saying, Let me not hear again the voice of Jehovah my God, neither let me see this great fire any more, that I die not. And Jehovah said unto me, They have well said that which they have spoken. I will raise them up a prophet from among their brethren, like unto thee; and I will put my words in his mouth, and he shall speak unto them all that I shall command him. And it shall come to pass, that whosoever will not hearken unto my words which he shall speak in my name, I will require it of him." (Deut. 18:15-19).[1]

How did Moses describe this prophet? *First,* he was not to speak with the fire and thunder which had accompanied the Lord's voice in Horeb when the Decalogue[2] covenant was given to Israel (Deut. 18:16; Ex. 19:9; 20:19-20). *Second,* the prophet was to be of Israel (Deut. 18:15, 18). *Third,* he was to be like Moses (Deut. 18:15). *Fourth,* God's word was to be in his mouth (Deut. 18:18). *Fifth,* the people would be held accountable, and thus those who refused to obey this prophet would have it required of them. They would suffer the consequences (Deut. 18:19).

---

[1] Note: unless otherwise noted, all quotations are from the American Standard Version (1901).

[2] The Ten Commandments.

ISRAEL WAS NOT TO ACCEPT JUST ANYONE

Just before Moses uttered the promise of the prophet to come, very strict warning was given to Israel to guard her against following false prophets. God's prophets were not like the imposters who in all ages have "traded upon human helplessness as regards the future" and upon human ignorance of divine things.[3] The nations around Israel had hearkened unto such false prophets, but Moses said:

> *"When thou art come into the land which Jehovah thy God giveth thee, thou shalt not learn to do after the abominations of those nations. There shall not be found with thee any one that maketh his son or his daughter to pass through the fire, one that useth divination, one that practiseth augury[4], or an enchanter, or a sorcerer, or a charmer, or a consulter with a familiar spirit, or a wizard, or a necromancer. For whosoever doeth these things is an abomination unto Jehovah: and because of these abominations Jehovah thy God doth drive them out from before thee. Thou shalt be perfect with Jehovah thy God. For these nations, that thou shalt dispossess, hearken unto them that practice augury, and unto diviners; but as for thee, Jehovah thy God hath not suffered thee so to do." (Deut. 18:9-14).*

They were not to resort to such characters as the diviners, and they were not to accept just everyone who came along and claimed to be a prophet of God. Those who claimed to be prophets of God were to be tested by what they *did* and by what they *taught*. If they

---

[3] William H. Thompson, *The Great Argument, or, Jesus Christ in the Old Testament*, New York: Harper and Brothers, 1884, pages 139-140.

[4] Uncertain meaning, though many state that it is a soothsayer who uses blood or other such means to "tell the future."

failed in the signs which they offered, they were to be rejected.

> *"But the prophet, which shall presume to speak a word in my name, which I have not commanded him to speak, or that shall speak in the name of other gods, that same prophet shall die. And if thou say in thine heart, How shall we know the word which the Lord hath not spoken? When a prophet speaketh in the name of the Lord, if the thing follow not, nor come to pass, that is the thing which the Lord hath not spoken, the prophet hath spoken it presumptuously, thou shalt not be afraid of him"* (Deut. 18:20-22).

On the other hand, if the prophet did give a sign which came to pass, but led them after other gods, they were to reject that prophet.

> *"If there arise in the midst of thee a prophet, or a dreamer of dreams, and give thee a sign or a wonder, and the sign or the wonder comes to pass, whereof he spake unto thee, saying, Let us go after other gods, which thou hast not known, and let us serve them; thou shall not hearken unto the words of that prophet, or unto that dreamer of dreams: for the Lord your God proveth you, to know whether ye love the Lord your God with all your heart and with all your soul.... And that prophet, or that dreamer of dreams, shall be put to death; because he hath spoken rebellion against Jehovah your God, who brought you out of the land of Egypt, and redeemed thee out of the house of bondage, to draw thee aside out of the way which the Lord thy God commanded thee to walk in. So shalt thou put away evil from the midst of thee."* (Deut. 13:1-5).

This was a serious matter, therefore God clearly warned Israel not to seek false prophets.

THE NEW TESTAMENT CLAIM

Peter quoted the prophecy and identified Christ as the prophet like unto Moses. To children of Israel he said:

> *"A prophet shall the Lord God raise up unto you from among your brethren, like unto me; to him shall ye hearken in all things whatsoever he shall speak unto you. And it shall be, that every soul that shall not hearken to that prophet, shall be utterly destroyed from among the people. Yea and all the prophets from Samuel and them that followed after, as many as have spoken, they also told of these days. Ye are the sons of the prophets, and of the covenant which God made with your fathers, saying unto Abraham, And in thy seed shall all the families of the earth be blessed. Unto you first, God, having raised up his Servant, sent him to bless you, in turning away every one of you from your iniquities."*
> *(Acts 3:22-26. Compare 7:37).*

It is clear that the New Testament claims that Christ is the prophet like unto Moses:

First, Christ is the prophet through whom God speaks to man today (Lk. 7:16; Heb. 1:1-2; 2:3-4). God's word is in His mouth (John 12:48-50; 17:8).

Second, Christ is an Israelite (Matt. 1:1-18).

Third, He is like Moses in that He is the mediator of a covenant, the great deliverer, the great teacher sent from God, and the lawgiver.

Fourth, His word is authoritative, and He has replaced Moses and Moses' covenant (Heb. 8:5-13; 12:24; 13:20; Matt. 17:1-8; 28:20).

Fifth, Men must hearken to Christ, or have it required of them (John 12:48).

Sixth, His Sermon on the Mount, and His deliverance of His new covenant, were free from the fire and terror-producing demonstrations which took place on Mount Sinai when the law was given (Deut. 18:16).

Seventh, He had a special nearness to God, and knew God face to face even more intimately than did Moses (Num. 12:6-8; Deut. 34:1-12; John 14:8-9; 1 Tim. 3:16).

Eighth, His ministry was interwoven with a host of miraculous demonstrations; just as was Moses' (Deut. 34:10-12).

The rest of this book deals with the question as to whether or not the claim—that Jesus is the prophet like unto Moses—can be sustained. The question is indeed serious, because if Christ is that prophet, we must hearken unto Him or have it required of us. We seek to be safe in our financial dealing, where only temporal and material losses are possible; how much more so should we endeavor to be safe where spiritual interests are at stake which concern both time and eternity!

CHAPTER 2

A Prophet Like Moses

Moses was the unique prophet of the Old Testament. What shows that the other prophets were not like him?

First, it is expressly said that his successors were not like him. If any of the successors of Moses were like Moses, surely Joshua would have been. God selected him (Num. 27:15-23). Moses himself had laid hands on Joshua. "And Joshua the son of Nun was full of the spirit of wisdom; for Moses had laid his hands upon him: and the children of Israel hearkened unto him, and did as Jehovah commanded Moses (Deut. 34:19). The people said that if God would be with Joshua, as He had been with Moses, they would obey Joshua, "And they answered Joshua, saying, All that thou hast commanded us we will do, and whithersoever thou sendest us we will go. According as we hearkened unto Moses in all things, so will we hearken unto thee: only Jehovah thy God be with thee, as he was with Moses (Joshua 1:16-18). In spite of such qualifications, Joshua was not a prophet like unto Moses, After Moses died, the people hearkened unto Joshua, in that they "did *as Jehovah commanded Moses,*" but we are expressly told that "there hath not arisen a prophet since in Israel like unto Moses..." (Deut. 34:9-12). Jehovah was with Joshua, but God emphasized that Joshua and the people had to "observe to do according to all the law, *which Moses my servant commanded thee:* turn not from it to the right hand or to the left.... This book of the law shall not depart out of thy mouth, but thou shalt meditate thereon day and night, that thou mayest observe to do according to all that is written therein..." (Joshua 1:5-9). Moses was still the lawgiver by whose law they were to live.

Second, Moses was unique because of the closeness of communion between him and God. After Moses died, we are told that "there hath not arisen a prophet since in Israel like unto Moses, *whom Jehovah knew face to face....*" (Deut. 34:10-11). Miriam and Aaron once spoke against Moses because of his marriage to the Cushite woman. "And they said, Hath Jehovah indeed spoken only with Moses? hath he not spoken with us?" (Num. 12:1, 2). Jehovah replied: "Hear now my words: if there be a prophet among you, I Jehovah will make myself known unto him in a vision. I will speak with him in a dream. My servant Moses is not so; he is faithful in all my house: with him will I speak mouth to mouth, even manifestly, and not in dark speeches; and the form of Jehovah shall he behold: wherefore then were ye not afraid to speak against my servant, against Moses?" (Num. 12:6-8).

Third, the miracles which confirmed the mission of Moses far surpassed that of all other prophets. We do not know exactly how long, but sometime after Moses' death it was written "there hath not arisen a prophet since in Israel like unto Moses, whom Jehovah knew face to face, *in all the signs and wonders,* which Jehovah sent him to do in the land of Egypt, to Pharaoh, and to all his servants, and to all his land, and in all the mighty hand, and in all the great terror, *which Moses wrought in the sight of all Israel.*" (Deut. 34:10-12).

Fourth, Moses differed from the other prophets in that he was the great lawgiver who gave the covenant to Israel. Moses was the mediator when God made His covenant with Israel (Deut. 5:5; 1 Kings 8:9, 21). The other prophets did not institute a new order of things but called on the people to hearken unto the law delivered by Moses. This was done by Nehemiah, Malachi and the other prophets (Neh. 8:1, 3, 7-8; Malachi 4:4).

Fifth, the uniqueness of Moses is also indicated by the fact that in Jesus' day, and today for that matter, the Old Testament was often divided into two sections: *Moses* and the prophets (Lk. 16:29,

30; 24:27, 44; Acts 26:22; 28:23).

JEWS VIEW MOSES AS UNIQUE

Jewish scholars recognize that Moses was distinct among the prophets. Maimonides (1135-1204 A.D.), who was also called Moses ben Maimon, was one of the outstanding rabbis. "Among the rabbis of the later Middle Ages and centuries thereafter, an adage was current, saying, 'From Moses to Moses there is none like unto Moses.' It means simply that Maimonides is to be regarded as the greatest figure in Jewish history since the man who delivered the Ten Commandments to the Jewish people. In fact, the spiritual development of Judaism up to the present age is incomprehensible without taking account of Maimonides' activities as a codifier, judge and commentator of the Bible and the Talmud."[1]

Although Maimonides seems to have interpreted Deut. 18:15-18 as the sending of an angel to the prophets, he maintained that Moses was unique in several ways.

First, "Here a principle is laid down which I have constantly expounded, viz., that all prophets except Moses received the prophecy through an angel. Note it."[2]

Second, God's relationship with Moses was more intimate than with the other prophets. Maimonides said: "That his prophecy was distinguished from that of all his predecessors is proved by the passage, 'And I appeared to Abraham, etc., but by my name, the Lord, I was not known unto them' (Ex. 6:3). We thus learn that his prophetic perception was different from that of the Patriarchs, and excelled it; *a fortiori*[3] it must have excelled that of other prophets

---

[1] Dagobert D. Runes, **Concise Dictionary of Judaism,** New York: Philosophical Library, 1959, p. 160. See also p. 172.

[2] Maimonides, *The Guide for the Perplexed,* New York: E. P. Dutton and Co., 1947, p. 223.

[3] Meaning, "And this is even stronger proof that…"

before Moses. As to the distinction of Moses' prophecy from that of succeeding prophets, it is stated as a fact, 'And there arose not a prophet since in Israel like unto Moses, whom the Lord knew face to face' (Deut. 34:10). It is thus clear that his prophetic perception was above that of later prophets in Israel, who are 'a kingdom of priests and a holy nation,' and 'in whose midst is the Lord'; much more it is above that of prophets among other nations."[4]

Yehezkel Kaufman pointed out that: "The prophetic ideal of the Bible is Moses (Deut. 34:10), of whom no ecstatic phenomena are ever related. To the contrary, the archetypal prophet speaks with God 'face to face, as a man speaks with his fellow' (Exod. 33:11); not in vision, dream, or riddle, but 'mouth to mouth' (Num. 12:6ff). God descends to speak with Moses at the entrance to the tent in the view of all the people, or calls to Moses and speaks with him from inside of the holy of holies."[5]

Third, Maimonides pointed out that Moses surpassed all other prophets with reference to the wonders which he wrought. The wonders of Moses, he argued, were witnessed by vast numbers of people and not just by a few individuals.[6]

Fourth, Maimonides and other Jewish scholars recognize that Moses differed from the other prophets in that he was the one through whom the covenant was given. Moses was "the lawgiver and 'master of the prophets.'" "Maimonides postulated the faith in the truth of Moses' prophecy (Moses' prophecy, but not Moses, the man) as one of the cardinal Jewish beliefs, summing up the Jewish consensus on Moses as follows: 'He was the master of all the prophets who preceded him, and those who followed him were all his inferiors'... Moses was the 'most perfect of all prophets and

---

[4] *Ibid.,* p. 224.

[5] Yehezkel Kaufmann, translated and abridged by Moshe Greenbert, **The Religion of Israel,** The University of Chicago Press, 1960, pp. 98-99.

[6] *Op. Cit.,* pp. 224-225.

teachers.'"[7] "The prophetic ideal of the Bible is Moses...,"[8] In other words, as Mowinckel pointed out, "Moses was the prophet *par excellence*, the pattern for all prophets."[9]

The fact that Moses' uniqueness is testified to both by the Old Testament and by Jewish scholars indicates that the prophet like unto Moses would not be like the other prophets.

"If we say of someone he's a scientist like Einstein, we're talking of one scientist, not of all of them. If we say of someone he's a president like Lincoln, we're talking of one president, not all of them. In each case we mean an individual. 'A prophet like me' means one person, or we eliminate a main point of what is said.

"'A scientist like Einstein' points to something unique in Einstein. 'A president like Lincoln' points to something unique in Lincoln. And 'a prophet like Moses' points to something unique in Moses that other prophets lacked."[10] The prophets whom God sent to Israel through the centuries were not like Moses. And yet, such a prophet was promised by Moses. Who was he and when did he come? Or *has* he come?

A GREAT PROPHET EXPECTED

In the first century there was an expectation that some great leader or leaders would arise. Tacitus, a Roman historian, in referring to the Jews said that "most had an implanted conviction, that it was contained in the ancient writings of the priests, that at that very time the East should prevail, and persons going forth out of Judaea should obtain the empire of the world, which ambiguities

[7] Trude Weiss-Rosmarin, *Judaism and Christianity: The Differences,* New York: The Jewish Book Club, 1943, p. 27.

[8] *Op. Cit.,* pp. 98-99.

[9] S. Mowinckel, *He That Cometh,* New York: Abingdon Press, 1954, p. 232.

[10] William F. Beck, "Like Moses," *The Lutheran News,* Nov. 28, 1966, p. 7.

had predicted Vespasian and Titus. But the common people, according to the wont of human cupidity,[11] interpreting in their own favor this exceeding fated greatness, were not turned to the truth even by adversity."[12] And Suetonius, also in the first century, wrote that "an ancient and settled opinion had become very prevalent in the whole East, that it was in the fates, that, at that time, persons going forth from Judaea should obtain the empire of the world. This, which (as the event subsequently showed) was predicted of the Roman Emperor, the Jews, drawing to themselves, rebelled."[13]

In the light of the promise of Moses, that a prophet like unto him would come, we are not surprised that Israel expected some great prophet. There were some who thought that Deut. 18:15 indicated "that Moses would come again."[14] However, Rabbi Levi ben Gerson remarked on Deut. 34:10 that: "Verily, the truth containing in this verse consists in that no prophet like Moses arose again, who was only a prophet in Israel; but there will come another who will also be a prophet of all the nations of the world, and the same is the King Messiah."[15]

THE NEW TESTAMENT RECORD

The New Testament records the expectation of a great prophet. In some cases the people seemed to identify this prophet with the Messiah, and in some cases they did not. When John the Baptist came preaching, "the Jews sent unto him from Jerusalem priests and Levites to ask him, Who art thou? And he confessed, and de-

---

[11] Greed for power, money, or possessions.

[12] *History*, V. 13.

[13] Vespasian, *Lives of the Twelve Caesars.*

[14] **S.** Mowinckel, ***op. cit.***, p. 299.

[15] Rabbi Levi ben Gerson, as quoted from his commentary on the books of Moses. Vol. 198, col. 2 by J. M. Hirschfelder, op. ***cit.***, p. 222.

nied not; I am not Christ. And they asked him, What then? Art thou Elijah? And he saith, I am not. Art thou the prophet? And he answered, No." (John 1:19-21). When Jesus wrought a miracle, the people said: "This is of a truth the prophet that cometh into the world." (John 6:14). On another occasion some said: "This is of a truth the prophet. Others said, This is the Christ. But some said, What, doth the Christ come out of Galilee?" (John 7:40-41).

There are other cases where the people seemed to identify the prophet and the Messiah as being the same person. The woman of Samaria perceived that Jesus was a prophet, and she also believed that when the Messiah came "He will declare unto us all things." (John 4:19, 25). Hirschfelder suggested that "the Samaritans base their Messianic hopes on this passage, rejecting all later prophecy, and interpret it as referring to a Messianic prophet."[16] Hengstenberg maintained that: "As the Samaritans acknowledged only the Pentateuch, there is no other passage than that under review from which the idea of the Messiah as a divinely enlightened teacher, which is here expressed, could have been derived. The last words agree in a remarkable manner with Deut. 18:18: 'And he shall speak unto them all that I shall command him.'"[17] Vincent Taylor acknowledged that the Samaritans expected a particular prophet, but denied it was current among the Jews.[18]

The people who wanted to make Jesus king by force seemed to view the prophet and the King Messiah as the same. "When therefore the people saw the sign which he did, they said, This of a truth is the prophet that cometh into the world. Jesus therefore perceiving that they were about to come and take him by force, to make

---

[16] Hirschfelder, *Messianic Prophecy*, page 112.

[17] E.W. Hengstenberg, *Christology of the Old Testament*, Grand Rapids, Michigan: Kregel Publications, Reprinted 1956, Vol. 1, page 106.

[18] Vincent Taylor, *The Names of Jesus*, London: The MacMillian Co., 1954, page 16.

him king, withdrew again into the mountain himself alone." (John 6:14-15).[19]

The way in which the prophecy is used in the New Testament indicates that the Messianic interpretation was the prevailing interpretation. Thus Peter and Stephen did not endeavor to prove that it was Messianic but argued from it as if the Messianic interpretation was the one which was held by the Jews to whom they appealed (Acts 3:22-23; 7:37). They identified the days of the prophet with the days of the Messiah (Acts 3:22, 24). That the common people looked for a great prophet is evident by the conclusion of the multitude who said of Jesus, after He had fed the multitudes with five loaves and two fishes, "This is of a truth the prophet that cometh into the world." (John 6:14).

To His enemies who were accusing Him, Jesus said:

> *"How can ye believe, who receive glory one of another, and the glory that cometh from the only God ye seek not? Think not that I will accuse you to the Father: there is one that accuseth you, even Moses, on whom ye have set your hope. For if ye believed Moses, ye would believe me; for he wrote of me. But if ye believe not his writings, how shall ye believe my words?" (John 5:44-47).*

Hengstenberg emphasized: "It is clear that the Lord must here have had in view a distinct passage of the Pentateuch—a clear and definite declaration of Moses... But if a single declaration—a direct Messianic prophecy—form the question at issue, our passage only can be meant; for it is the only prophecy of Christ which Moses, on whose person great stress is laid, uttered in his own name. Moreover, Christ would more readily expect that the Jews would

---

[19] Compare Mowinckel, *op. cit.*, page 302. He thinks that they were identifying the prophet, who was to be the Messiah's forerunner, with the Messiah.

acknowledge our prophecy to be fulfilled in Him, than the prophecy in Gen. 49, which refers rather to the Messiah in glory. The preceding words of Jesus likewise contain references to the passage now under consideration. Verse 38—'And ye have not His word abiding in you; for whom He hath sent, Him ye believe not'—contains an allusion to Deut. 18:18: 'And I will put My words into his mouth, and he shall speak unto them all that I shall command him;' so that whosoever rejects the Ambassador of God, rejects His word at the same time. John 5:43: 'I am come in My Father's name, and ye receive Me not,' acquires both its significance and earnestness from its reference to verse 19 of our passage: 'Whosoever will not hearken unto My words, which he shall speak in My name, I will require it of him.' *Further*—The point at issue in this discourse of Christ is an accusation of the Jews against Christ, that He had violated the Mosaic law (Compare John 5:10-16, and verse 18, which states the second apparent violation of the law). It was thus highly appropriate that Jesus should throw back upon the Jews the charge which they brought against Him, and should prove to them that it was just they who were in fatal opposition to the enactments of the Mosaic law. *Finally*—It is this same Moses in whom they trusted, whom they considered as their patron, and whom to please the more, they were so zealous for his law against Jesus—it is this same Moses whom Jesus represents as their accuser. And he is such an accuser as renders every other superfluous, so that Christ did not need specially to come forward in such a character. The accusation of Moses must, then, according to this declaration, and in accordance with what follows, refer to the cause of Christ. But the passage under review is the only Messianic prophecy of a *threatening character* which the Pentateuch contains; the only one in which divine judgments are threatened to the despisers of the Messiah—the only Mosaic foundation for the denunciation: 'Woe to the people that despiseth thee.' If it be denied that Christ refers to it—if its Messianic character be not acknowledged, the first words of Christ are destitute of foundation."[20]

Christ also equates God's word with His word when he claimed that He had received the word from the Father and that men would be held responsible and be judged if they rejected his word (John 12:48-50).

We believe that the evidence justifies Thomson's conclusion that "it is a fact of history that the whole Hebrew race regarded the relation of Moses to it as so exceptional that no subsequent personage, prophet, priest, or king, was ever supposed by it to be like unto him in office or position. The consistent testimony of the nation shows that to the Hebrew mind the conception of the coming of one like unto Moses would also convey the intimation of another great national exigency[21], at least equal in importance to the deliverance from the Bondage. Moses was not only the prophet of the nation, but its sole founder, statesman, and legislator. It was therefore natural that this Mosaic prophecy should early have come to be regarded as an especial and important prediction of the advent of the Messiah, and as a pledge of the survival of Israel unto his coming."[22]

---

[20] *Ibid.*, pages 107-108.

[21] An urgent need, or something requiring immediate action.

[22] Thompson, *op. cit.,* pages 143-144.

CHAPTER 3

The Two Mediators

Moses was the mediator of the Old Testament. He stood between Israel and God. God had spoken to Moses "face to face as when one talks with a friend" (Ex. 33:11). When the law was being delivered on the mount, the people were frightened. Moses said, concerning the Ten Commandments, "These words Jehovah spake unto all your assembly in the mount out of the midst of the fire, of the cloud, and of the thick darkness, with a great voice: and he added no more. And he wrote them upon two tables of stone, and gave them unto me. And it came to pass, when ye heard the voice out of the midst of the darkness, while the mountain was burning with fire, that ye came near unto me, even all the heads of your tribes, and your elders; and ye said, Behold Jehovah our God hath showed us his glory and his greatness, and we have heard his voice out of the midst of the fire: we have seen this day that God doth speak with men, and he liveth. Now therefore why should we die? for this great fire will consume us: if we hear the voice of Jehovah our God any more then we shall die. For who is there of all flesh, that hath heard the voice of the living God speaking out of the midst of the fire, as we have and lived? Go thou near, and hear all that Jehovah our God shall **say:** and speak thou unto us all that Jehovah our God shall speak unto thee, and we will hear it, and do it. And Jehovah heard the voice of your words, when you spake unto me; and Jehovah said unto me, I have heard the voice of the words of this people, which they have spoken unto thee: they have well said all that they have spoken." (Deut. 5:22-28).

As a result of this, Moses told the people that: "I stood between Jehovah and you at that time, to show you the word of Jehovah; for ye were afraid because of the fire, and went not up into the mount." (Deut. 5:5).

> *"And it came to pass, when Moses came down from Mount Sinai with the two tables of the testimony in Moses' hand, when he came down from the mount, that Moses knew not that the skin of his face shone by reason of his speaking with him. And when Aaron and all the children of Israel saw Moses, behold, the skin of his face shone; and they were afraid to come nigh him. And Moses called unto them; and Aaron and all the rulers of the congregation returned unto him: and Moses spake to them. And afterward all the children of Israel came nigh: and he gave them in commandment all that Jehovah had spoken with him in Mount Sinai. And when Moses had done speaking with them, he put a veil on his face." (Ex. 34:29-33).*

Through Moses the mediator, God made a covenant with Israel "in the day that I took them by the hand to bring them out of the land of Egypt" (Jer. 31:32). This was the Decalogue covenant, for the Ten Commandments constituted the foundation of God's agreement with Israel. Thus we are told that: "There was nothing in the ark save the two tables of stone which Moses put there at Horeb..." "And there have I set a place for the ark, wherein is the covenant of Jehovah, which he made with our fathers, when he brought them out of the land of Egypt." (1 Kings 8:9, 21).

The prophets who came after Moses did not institute a covenant; instead they called Israel back to the covenant which Moses had mediated. Thus, in Nehemiah's day, Ezra the scribe brought forth and read to the people "the book of the law of Moses, which Jehovah had commanded to Israel" (Neh. 8:1). Centuries later Malachi said: "Remember ye the law of Moses my servant, which I commanded unto him in Horeb for all Israel, even statutes and or-

23

dinances." (Mal. 4:4).

MOSES TO BE SUPERSEDED

Although Moses was the great prophet of the Old Testament, Moses and some of the other prophets indicated that Moses would be superseded. Jeremiah indicated that Moses would be superseded. Israel had disobeyed the old covenant which had been given through Moses. God said that He would make a new covenant which would be unlike the old. Since the old was the one made through Moses (Jer. 31:31-35; 1 Kings 8:9, 21), and since it was to be abolished, Moses the mediator would give way to whoever mediated the new covenant. As long as Moses' authority stood, the old law could not be abolished. But the fact that it was to be abolished indicated that Moses' authority, and his mediatorship, would come to an end. But a covenant could not be instituted without being instituted through a prophet of God. This prophet would have to have the authority to abolish Moses' covenant. And since this prophet would establish the covenant, he would be a mediator between God and man. Such a prophet would indeed be a prophet like unto Moses for he, too would be a mediator. None of the other Old Testament prophets were mediators in the sense that Moses was, for none of them established a covenant as did Moses. The One who superseded Moses would be one who was like unto Moses in that he would be the mediator of a covenant.

Professor Kurtz pointed out that: "Now a prophet like *unto Moses,* must necessarily, like him, be a redeemer of the people a founder and executor of a new covenant with God; and since a new covenant is, by implication, better than that which preceded it, it follows that the prophet, who is like unto Moses is thus really *a greater* than he is. Hence this prophecy applied in its fullness to no prophet of the old covenant. It is in Christ alone, the executor of the new covenant, the Redeemer of all men, that this promise is perfectly and finally fulfilled."[1]

The fact that the covenant of Moses would be superseded was indicated in David's prophecy of the Messiah who was to be both king and priest on his throne. His priesthood was to be after the order of Melchizedek (Psa. 110:1, 4). As long as Moses' covenant stood, the temple system and its priesthood were binding. Messiah the king was to come from the tribe of Judah, but the priests were from the tribe of Levi. David prophesied that the Messiah-King would be a priest after the order of Melchizedek and thus not after the order of Aaron. The priesthood was to be changed, and thus the law itself was to be changed. The change of the law regarding priesthood necessitated a change of the covenant itself, for the Levitical priesthood was part and parcel of the Mosaic system.

Moses himself indicated that he was to be superseded when he prophesied that God would raise up a prophet like unto him (Deut. 18:15-18). The test of their obedience to God would be whether or not they obeyed the prophet like unto Moses. When Moses said that when this prophet comes you are to hearken to him, Moses was saying that the prophet was to be the authority.

"That that great prophet should speak things different from what Moses had spoken or would speak, is very evident from the fact that God makes their obedience or disobedience—not to Moses, but to that great prophet, when he should appear—the measure of their accountability to him. This Scripture does not say or in any way indicate that the prophet was to bring them back to the law written by Moses; but plainly indicates a prophet in authority, like Moses. Now, Moses was both a deliverer, a mediator and a lawgiver. The plain inference is that that prophet was, in some important sense, to supersede Moses; and, if to be like him, would

---

[1] As quoted by J. M. Hirschfelder, op. cit., p. 224.

also be a deliverer and a lawgiver."[2]

"If this is all true, and I think it is, it strongly implies a release from the authority of Moses, and the assumption of a corresponding new obligation to hearken to that great prophet, when he should appear with a new and different message. This is further corroborative from the fact that none of the prophets who followed in Israel for the succeeding thousand years, closing with Malachi—none of them ever assumed to be that great prophet; but all taught the Law of Moses faithfully. The prophet Jeremiah, however, indicates a time in the future when God, in fact would make a *new covenant* with Israel, and, of course, the new must necessarily differ from the old, else there would or could be no necessity for it; but, upon the authority of Jeremiah, the *new* was not to be *like the old*."[3]

Concerning the significance of being like Moses, and being the one unto whom the people were to hearken, Cairns wrote: "... the emphasis must have been laid upon a true Equal, one who should make a new beginning, and speak with the commanding authority which he alone possessed. Hence this view impressed itself on the whole Old Testament Church—as we see in the latest oracle of Malachi, and as is vouched for by the New Testament taken simply as a human document, recording among Jews and Samaritans the expectation of a transcendent Teacher and Reformer, such as the world had but once seen before. Indeed, in the circumstances of the case, to be equal to Moses was to be greater for if Moses was simply repeated, what need of another lawgiver or founder? How, then, can the denier of revelation account for these facts: *First,* for the expectation ascribed to Moses, and *secondly,* for its fulfillment? The very desire and anticipation were singular. Great men

---

[2] William Ruble, Letters to the Literal Children of Abraham, Cincinnati: F. L. Rowe Publishers, 1911, pp. 6-7.

[3] Ibid., p. 7.

do not usually subordinate themselves to others, or think of their work as waiting on some greater personality, who is to take up its unfinished issues. The Christian scheme of things accounts for this in Moses, who looked not only for a kindred spirit but for a personal Savior, whose work was more than the sequel of his own. And still more wonderful is the realization of this hope, which after fifteen centuries arrived: for the prevailing opinion even of the world is that Christ is of the same mould with Moses, only greater and more commanding working in the same element, and making the work of Moses, which seemed exhausted or defeated, renew and exalt itself in His own."[4]

This did not mean that the prophet like unto Moses perpetuated Moses work, for he would not have been like Moses if he had simply called the people back to the Law of Moses. Instead the prophet like unto Moses fulfilled what Moses and the Old Testament prophets predicted with reference to the Christ and the new covenant (Matt. 5:17-18).

At least some of the Jewish rabbis recognized that the law would be done away, or at least certain parts of it—such as the ceremonial law—would be abolished. But to abolish a part of the Law of Moses would mean that the authority of Moses had been superseded by one superior to Moses; for as long as Moses was authoritative his law was to be obeyed. Thus the Midrash in its interpretation of Isa. 52:13 maintained that the Messiah would be greater than Moses. "The celebrated commentator Abarbanel, in his commentary on the minor prophets, states that there was a common saying among the ancient Hebrews, that 'the Messiah shall be exalted above Abraham, lifted up above Moses, and higher than the angels of the ministry.'"[5]

---

[4] Cairns, "The Present State of the Christian Argument From Prophecy," *Present Day Tracts*, London, England.

[5] As quoted by Hirschfelder, op. cit., p. 222.

27

Some rabbis maintained that "The commandments will be annulled in the future." The Messiah would give a new law which would replace the old law. Midrash Tehillim has a homily on Psalm 146:7 which indicates that at least some aspects of the ceremonial law would be abolished, and therefore some things which had been forbidden would then be allowed. In his comments on this homily, Dr. A. Stanley Dreyfus said: "Our homily then is in agreement with Paul, and both are representative of certain Jewish views regarding the eventual abrogation of Torah This Midrash cannot be considered a Christian interpolation."[6]

The abolition of the law, however, would have to be done by God through a prophet or messenger. And the one who abrogated the law would have to be greater in authority than Moses who had given the law. He would have to have the authority in God to end the Law of Moses. This is but another way of saying that he would have the authority to end the mediatorship of Moses through ending his covenant. Is not this the very thing which one would expect from a prophet who was like unto Moses, and would not a prophet have to be like unto Moses as a lawgiver or covenant-maker in order to abolish Moses' law?

INTERCESSOR

Moses was not only the mediator but he also interceded for the people. S. Mowinckel observed that "an important element in the tradition about Moses is his constant intercession for the sinful people. He is even ready to die, in order to appease the wrath of Yahweh against the people; and the punishment for their sins falls on him as well."[7] When Moses was in the mount the people cor-

---

[6] Dr. A. Stanley Dreyfus, "Paul, The Rabbis and The Abrogation of the Law," p. 7. Mimeographed article.

[7] S. Mowinckel, He That Cometh, New York: Abingdon Press, 1954, p. 232. Translated by G. W. Anderson.

rupted themselves with idolatry and immorality. God's wrath was kindled against them. "And Moses besought Jehovah his God, and said, Jehovah, why doth thy wrath wax hot against thy people, that thou hast brought forth out of the land of Egypt with great power and with a mighty hand?" (Ex. 32:11). Moses returned to the people and said: "Ye have sinned a great sin: and now I will go up unto Jehovah; peradventure I shall make atonement for your sins. And Moses returned unto Jehovah, and said, Oh, this people have sinned a great sin, and have made them gods of gold. Yet now, if thou wilt forgive their sins—; and if not, blot me, I pray thee, out of thy book which thou hast written." (Ex. 32:30-32).

As great as he was, Moses could not bear the sins of the people. The prophet like unto Moses, however, did both intercede for the people and bore their sins. Isaiah foresaw this work of Christ. Therefore, long before Jesus came, Isaiah wrote:

"Surely he hath borne our griefs, and carried our sorrows; yet we did esteem him stricken, smitten of God, and afflicted. But he was wounded for our transgressions, he was bruised for our iniquities; the chastisement of our peace was upon him; and with his stripes we are healed. All we like sheep have gone astray; we have turned every one to his own way; and Jehovah hath laid on him the iniquity of us all.... By oppression and judgment he was taken away; and as for his generation, who among them considered that he was cut off out of the land of the living for the transgression of my people to whom the stroke was due?... He shall see of the travail of his soul, and shall be satisfied: by the knowledge of himself shall my righteous servant justify many; and he shall bear their iniquities. Therefore will I divide him a portion with the great, and he shall divide the spoil with the strong; because he poured out his soul unto death, and was num-

bered with the transgressors: yet he bare the sin of many, and made intercession for the transgressors." (Isa. 53:4-6, 8, 11-12).

"Wherefore also he is able to save to the uttermost them that draw near unto God through him, seeing he ever liveth to make intercession for them. For such a high priest became us, holy, guileless, undefiled, separated from sinners, and made higher than the heavens; who needeth not daily, like those high priests, to offer up sacrifices, first for his own sins, and then for the sins of the people; for this he did once for all, when he offered up himself." (Heb. 7:25-27).

He alone, of all the prophets, is our mediator because He is our redeemer. "For there is one God, one mediator also between God and man, himself man, Christ Jesus, who gave himself a ransom for all...." (1 Tim. 2:5-6).

THE CIRCUMSTANCES TO DIFFER

Moses told the people that the circumstances surrounding the deliverance of the word of the prophet like unto him would differ from those at the giving of the law. What had Israel desired of Jehovah "in Horeb in the day of the assembly?" They had said: "Let me not hear again the voice of Jehovah my God, neither let me see this great fire any more, that I die not." (Deut. 18:16). What had been Moses' position at the time these things occurred? He had stood between them and God, and God spoke to Moses so that the people could hear God and believe Moses. In preparation for the deliverance of the Ten Commandments, "Jehovah said unto Moses, Lo, I come unto thee in a thick cloud, that *the people may hear when I speak with thee,* and may also believe thee for ever." (Ex. 19:9). Moses told the people these words (Ex. 19:9), and Jehovah then told Moses to prepare the people "and be ready against the third day; for the third day Jehovah will come down in the sight of all the people upon Mount Sinai" (19:11). The people were not to touch the mount, although they were to come "up to the mount" (19:13).

> *"And it came to pass on the third day, when it was morning, that there were thunders and lightnings, and a thick cloud upon the mount, and the voice of a trumpet exceeding loud; and all the people that were in the camp trembled. And Moses brought forth the people out of the camp to meet God; and they stood at the nether part of the mount. And Mount Sinai, the whole of it, smoked, because Jehovah descended upon it in fire; and the smoke thereof ascended as the smoke of a furnace, and the whole mount quaked greatly. And when the voice of the trumpet waxed louder and louder, Moses spake, and God answered him by a voice" (Ex. 19:16-19).*

Then Jehovah called Moses to the top of the mount, and later the Lord sent him back to the people. Afterwards Moses was to come back up with Aaron. Moses told these things to the people and the Lord then spake the words of the Ten Commandments (Ex. 19:20-20:1). However, even when Jehovah was speaking to the people, Moses was their mediator for he stood between them and God. As Moses later said concerning the words of the covenant, which God spoke to the people, that "Jehovah spake with you face to face in the mount out of the midst of the fire, (I stood between Jehovah and you at that time to show you the word of Jehovah: for ye were afraid because of the fire, and went not up into the mount;) saying…" (Deut. 5:4-5). And then came the Decalogue. Their fear, and Moses standing between them and God, was manifested when they first came to the mount and God spoke to the people (Ex.

19:16).

When the Ten Commandments were spoken, the people were so frightened that they "said unto Moses, Speak thou with us, and we will hear; but let not God speak with us, lest we die." (Ex. 20:19). They also said: "Go thou near, and hear all that Jehovah our God shall say: and speak thou unto us all that Jehovah our God shall speak unto thee; and we will hear it, and do it," (Deut. 5:27). Jehovah agreed to their request, and then exhorted them to fear Him, and keep all of His commandments, statutes, and ordinances which He would give through Moses. They were not to turn "aside to the right hand or to the left. Ye shall walk in all the way which Jehovah your God hath commanded you, that ye may live, and that it may be well with you, and that ye may prolong your days in the land which ye shall possess." (Deut. 5:32-33).

In all of this, even when God spoke to them out of the mount (Deut. 5:4), Moses was the mediator who stood between them and God. When he received from God the Decalogue on the two tables of stone he received them for the people (Deut. 5:22). When Moses promised them another prophet he reminded them of the request which they had made at Sinai (Deut. 18:16). This, too, is fulfilled in Christ. The deliverance of His word in His personal ministry, and through His apostles and prophets after His ascension, was not accompanied by the fear-producing demonstrations that took place at Sinai.

DELIVERER

Moses was the great deliverer of Israel from bondage in Egypt as well as bondage to ignorance and sin. In speaking of Moses' position in the history of Israel, Joseph Klausner wrote: "The name Moses (Heb. *Mosheh*) itself, according to popular etymology, indicates one who brings out or ransoms. The Talmud calls him 'savior of Israel.'" It was "inevitable that the people should feel compelled to accord the very greatest glory and honor to the exalted and grandiose personality of *the first deliverer.* This was the man Moses, the great deliverer, who not only ransomed Israel from all its material troubles and from *political* servitude, but also redeemed it from its ignorance and its spiritual bondage. He was not only a guide and leader of the Israelite peoples; he was also a lawgiver and prophet. The exalted picture of Moses necessarily, therefore, impressed itself upon the spirit of the nation and became a symbol of the redeemer in general. Political salvation and spiritual redemption of necessity were combined in the consciousness of the nation to become one great work of redemption. Thus was born the redemptive dualism which necessarily put its stamp upon the redeemer of the future, *the expected Messiah."*

"The authors of the Talmud and Midrash, with their fine national feeling, perceived the relation and connection between the Messianic expectation and the exodus from Egypt, between the Messiah and Moses. They name Moses 'the first redeemer' in contrast to the Messiah, who is 'the last redeemer.'"[8]

Moses rescued Israel from Egyptian bondage, while Christ is the Savior of the world—both Jews and Gentiles. Moses delivered Israel from slavery, and Christ delivers us from slavery to sin. "Moses appointed the Passover lamb to be sacrificed without breaking its bones; its blood protected the people from destruction. Jesus is God's Passover Lamb; His bones were not broken; and His blood protects us. When snakes bit people and they were dying, Moses raised a copper snake on a kind of cross; those who looked at it were healed. Jesus put Himself on the cross: look at Him and be healed." "Moses gave his people a covenant and dedicated it with blood." "And Moses took the blood, and sprinkled it on the

---

[8] The Messianic Idea in Israel, New York: The MacMillan Co., 1955, pp. 15-16, 17. Translated by W. F. Stinespring. Compare John Gill, Commentary on Acts, 3:22.

people, and said, Behold the blood of the covenant, which Jehovah hath made with you concerning all these words." (Ex. 24:8). Jesus gave His own blood as the blood of the covenant (Matt. 26:28). "Moses brought the people to the Jordan beyond which lay the land of milk and honey."[9] Christ promised to come again and receive the faithful unto Himself in the eternal home (John 14:3).

Christ is not only the great deliverer from sin, but as His principles work in the hearts of men He also brings increasing freedom to man in all aspects of life; including the political. Of all the Israelites who have lived since Moses' day, Christ is the one who is pre-eminently like Moses in being the great mediator, intercessor, and deliverer.

---

[9] William F. Beck, "Like Moses", The Lutheran News, Nov. 28, 1966, p. 7

CHAPTER 4

The New Covenant

Jeremiah prophesied that God would establish a new covenant which would be unlike the old covenant. The old was made with Israel when God brought them out of Egypt. Moses was its mediator (Jer. 31:31-34; 1 Kings 8:9, 21).

OLD COVENANT TO BE ABOLISHED

Jeremiah said that the old covenant would be abolished. Furthermore, he said Israel had not kept it (Jer. 31:31-32). Jeremiah did not say that God would write *the old covenant* in a new *place*, so that the difference would be that instead of being written on stone the same covenant would be written on hearts. Jeremiah said that God would make a new *covenant*. God did not say that He would make a new *people* who would keep the old covenant. While it is true that those with whom the new covenant would be made would be a new people, yet God said that he would make a new covenant. He not only said that it would be new, but He further underscored this fact by saying that *it would be unlike the old covenant*, which was the Mosaic covenant. "I will make a *new covenant...not* according to the covenant that I made with their fathers in the day that I took them by the hand to bring them out of the land of Egypt; which my covenant they brake, although I was a husband unto them, saith Jehovah." (Jer. 31:31-32). He then proceeded to describe some aspects of the newness of the new covenant (Jer. 31:33-34).[1]

---

[1] On some of the differences in the covenants see James D. Bales, *Messiah's Mission* and *The New Covenant Is New*.

THE OLD COVENANT HAS BEEN ABOLISHED

When God said that He would make a new covenant, unlike the old, He made it clear that the old was temporary. Has the old covenant been abolished? The New Testament teaches that it has been abolished (Heb. 8:6-13; 12:24). Although Jews as a people do not accept the New Testament, they must accept the fact that the old covenant has long ago been abolished. It was a local covenant, for one nation, which would give way to a universal covenant. As Richard Whately pointed out:

"We have the most satisfactory reasons for believing that the Law of Moses was given by divine command; and also that it was given to the one nation of Israel, and not designed for the rest of mankind.

"One of the many marks one may perceive of this design is: that it was a *local* religion. The Israelites were directed to offer sacrifices, and to worship three times a year, at the one 'place which the Lord should choose to set his name there' (that is, to place there the manifestation of his presence and power); and they were strictly forbidden to sacrifice anywhere else (Deut. 12:13-14). And accordingly, when the Temple at Jerusalem had been finally fixed on as the chosen place, the destruction of that Temple made it thenceforth impossible for an Israelite to keep up the chief ordinances of his religion.

"Hence the final destruction of that Temple abolished, manifestly and totally, the Mosaic system of religion.

"And it is very remarkable that that religion is almost the only one that could have been abolished against the will of the people themselves, and while they resolved firmly to maintain it. Their religion, and theirs only, could be, and has been, thus abolished in spite of their firm attachment to it, on account of its being dependent on a particular place. The Christian religion, or again, any of the pagan religions, could not be abolished by any force of enemies, if the persons professing the religion were sincere and resolute in keeping to it. To destroy a Christian place of worship, or to turn it into a Mohammedan mosque (as was done in many instances by the Turks), would not prevent the exercise of the Christian religion. And even if Christianity were forbidden by law, and Christians persecuted (as has in times past been so frequently done), still they might assemble secretly in woods or caves, or they might fly to foreign countries to worship God, according to their own faith; and Christianity, though it might be driven out of one country, would still exist in others.

"And the same may be said of the pagan religions. If it happened that any temple of Jupiter, or Diana, or Woden, were destroyed, this would not hinder the worshippers of those gods from continuing to worship them as before, and from offering sacrifices to them elsewhere.

"But it was not so with the Jews. Their religion was so framed as to make the observance of its ordinances impossible, when their Temple was finally destroyed. It seems to have been designed and contrived by divine providence, that as their law was to be brought to an end by the Gospel (for which it was a preparation), so, all men were to perceive that it did come to an end, notwithstanding the obstinate rejection of the Gospel by the greater part of the Jews. It was not left to be a question and a matter of opinion, whether the sacrifices instituted by Moses were to be continued or not; but things were so ordered as to put it out of man's power to continue them."[2]

---

[2] Richard Whately, Rise, *Progress, and Corruptions of Christianity*, pp. 67-69.

IT CANNOT BE RE-ESTABLISHED BY ISRAEL

Not only has the old covenant been abolished, but it is impossible for Israel to decide to keep the old covenant and to enter again into this covenant relationship with God. *First,* one cannot unilaterally enter into a covenant with someone else. A covenant involves the decision of the two parties between whom the covenant is made. If one party breaks the covenant, the covenant ends. The party who has broken the covenant cannot then unilaterally re-establish the covenant. Has the covenant been broken?

(a) God said that Israel had not kept the covenant, although God had been faithful to His covenant relationship with them (b) As a matter of historical fact, for some two thousand years Israel has not kept the covenant. The temple no longer exists, and its sacrifices have not been offered for centuries. So it is obvious that both the Old Testament and history say that Israel has not continued in the covenant.

Second, the priestly line has long been broken. Unless the priestly line could be traced with certainty, an individual could not officiate as a priest. Thus genealogies were kept in order to ensure the purity of the priestly line (Ezra 2:62). Josephus, a Jewish historian of the first century, wrote that "he who is partaker of the priesthood must propagate of a wife of the same nation, without having any regard to money, or any other dignities; but he is to make a scrutiny, and take his wife's genealogy from the ancient tables, and procure many witnesses to it. And this is our practice not only in Judea, but wheresoever any body of men of our nation do live; and even there an exact catalogue of our priests' marriages is kept; I mean at Egypt and at Babylon, or any other place of the rest of the habitable earth, whithersoever our priests are scattered; for they send to Jerusalem the ancient names of their parents in writing, as well as those of their remoter ancestors, and signify who are the witnesses also. But if any war falls out, such as have

38

fallen out a great many of them already, when Antiochus Epiphanes made an invasion upon our country, as when Pompey the Great and Quintilius Varus did so also, and principally in the wars that have happened in our own times, those priests that survive them compose new tables of genealogy out of the old records, and examine the circumstances of the records, and examine the circumstances of the women that remain; for still they do not admit of those that have been captives, as suspecting that they had conversation with some foreigners. But what is the strongest argument of our exact management in this matter is what I am now going to say, that we have the names of our high priests from father to son set down in our records, for the interval of two thousand years; and if any of these have been transgressors of these rules, they are prohibited to present themselves at the altar, or to be partakers of any other of our purifications: and this is justly, or rather necessarily done, because every one is not permitted of his own accord to be a writer, nor is there any disagreement in what is written; they being only prophets that have written the original and earliest account of things, as they learned them of God himself by inspiration; and others have written what hath happened in their own times, and that in a very distinct manner also."[3]

Even if the nation of Israel were to build a temple today, they would not have the power to re-enter the covenant, and they could not know who the priests were to be. The genealogies have been destroyed and no one can trace with certainty the descendants of the tribe of Levi. Who can know who today is a descendant of Aaron?

It may be replied that Israel wanted to continue in the covenant; and it was not her fault that Jerusalem was destroyed in A.D. 70, the nation scattered, and the priestly line lost. To this we an-

---

[3] Josephus, *Against Apion*, Book I, Paragraph 7, p. 861.

swer: (a) God said that Israel had broken the covenant (Jer. 31:31-34) (b) If God had wanted Israel to have continued in the covenant He would have made it possible for her to have done so (c) Captivities, such as the Babylonian, were judgments of God on Israel. But Israel has been scattered, the temple has been destroyed, and the covenant has been unkept for many centuries longer than any of the judgments of God on Israel in the Old Testament. How can Israel avoid the conclusion that this has been a judgment of God on Israel? And, if it is a judgment of God, what happened in her history that was even more of a rebellion against God than the sin of idolatry; for which and related sins Israel was taken into captivity during Old Testament days? Why this much longer judgment of God on Israel? What is God trying to tell Israel in this judgment? She is being told that she was cut off because of unbelief and this because of her failure to hearken to the prophet like unto Moses (Rom 11:20-23; Deut. 18:19).

A PROPHET LIKE UNTO MOSES NECESSARY

A new covenant could not be instituted without being instituted through some prophet of God. He would have to be like Moses, for Moses instituted a covenant. The prophet who did it would have to have authority which enabled him to supersede Moses and his covenant, If that prophet did not have authority to set aside Moses and his covenant, a new covenant could not possibly be established. The fact that the new covenant was to be established proves that the old was temporary and that it would have to give way to make room for the new covenant.

NOT MADE WITH ISRAEL?

It may be maintained that although Jesus did establish a covenant, it could not be the covenant prophesied by Jeremiah, for Jeremiah said that it would be made with Judah and with Israel (Jer.

31:31-32). To this we reply: *First,* a covenant, which involves an agreement between two parties, cannot be entered into unilaterally by one party. God does not unilaterally enter into a covenant with man, and thus He does not make a covenant with anyone who is unwilling for the covenant to be made with him. Even though the old covenant was made with Israel as a nation, those within the nation who did not keep the terms of the national covenant were considered to be in violation of the covenant, and if they continued in disobedience the covenant relationship was broken. But even with the nation of Israel, God would not have entered the covenant if the nation itself had been unwilling. Therefore the new covenant would not be made with any of Judah and Israel who refused to accept it. The possibility of disobedience was implied by Moses when he said that those who did not hear the prophet would have it required of them (Deut. 18:19).

Second, both Israel's history and prophecy emphasize that not all of fleshly Israel was included in the promises of God. Paul raised the question as to how the promises of God could be fulfilled in Christ even though the nation of Israel as a whole had rejected Jesus Christ. Paul dealt with this problem from several standpoints.

(a) The promises of God did not embrace all physical descendants of Abraham just because they were Abraham's descendants. In other words, not all of physical Israel is true Israel. Thus Paul wrote: "But it is not as though the word of God hath come to nought. For they are not all Israel, that are of Israel: neither, because they are Abraham's seed, are they all children: but, in Isaac shall thy seed be called. That is, it is not the children of the flesh that are children of God; but the children of the promise are reckoned for a seed." (Rom. 9:6-8). Ishmael was a descendant of Abraham, but God's promise was that "in Isaac shall thy seed be called." To come within the scope of God's blessings one must come under His promises and whatever conditions, if any, God has made with reference to those promises. For Israel to be in the new covenant, and enjoy its promises, it is necessary for her to accept the covenant. It is not sufficient to be of physical Israel.

(b) Israel's history reveals that in many cases the nation as a whole was unfaithful and that it was but a remnant which accepted the message of God. Because God cast off the disobedient, it did not mean that He cast off those who actually continued to be His people. Thus in Elijah's day there was a remnant (Rom. 11:2-4). Isaiah had foreseen that it was a remnant which would be saved, even though the number of physical Israelites was much greater. "And Isaiah crieth concerning Israel, If the number of the children of Israel be as the sand of the sea, it is the remnant that shall be saved: for the Lord will execute his word upon the earth, finishing it and cutting it short. And, as Isaiah hath said before, except the Lord of Sabaoth had left us a seed, We had become as Sodom, and had been made like unto Gomorrah." (Rom. 9:27-29). The Israel whom God foreknew was the Israel which was *willing,* and not all of physical Israel. Paul showed that his own conversion was a part of the proof that the covenant had been made with a remnant. "I say then, Did God cast off his people? God forbid. For I also am an Israelite, of the seed of Abraham, of the tribe of Benjamin. God did not cast off his people which he foreknew. Or know ye not what the scripture saith of Elijah? how he pleadeth with God against Israel: Lord, they have killed thy prophets, they have digged down thine altars; and I am left alone, and they seek my life. But what saith the answer of God unto him? I have left for myself seven thousand men, who have not bowed the knee to Baal. Even so then at this present time there also is a remnant according to the election of grace" (Rom. 11:1-5). The new covenant was made with thousands of Israelites. On the first Pentecost after Christ's resurrection the apostles preached to Jews and proselytes (Acts 2:5, 10). "Men of Judea" and "men of Israel" were addressed (Acts 2:14, 22). The conclusion, which was established by various lines of argument, was: "*Let all the house of Israel* therefore know assuredly, that God hath made him both Lord and Christ, this Jesus whom ye crucified" (Acts 2:36). Through Christ the covenant was offered to all. That day around three thousand obeyed the gospel (Acts 2:33-41). As time went on many more did likewise (Acts 4:32; 5:14; 6:1, 7). Thus with a remnant of physical Israel the covenant was established. What happened to the rest? They were cut off because of their unbelief (Rom. 11:20). Moses himself taught that God would require it of those who did not obey the prophet like unto Moses (Deut. 18:19).

(c) Paul also showed that the prophets had foreseen and foretold Israel's disobedience. In Zion there was "a stone of stumbling and a rock of offence" (Rom, 9:33; Isa. 28:16). As Paul said, and backed up what he said with Old Testament statements: "But they did not all hearken to the glad tidings. For Isaiah saith, Lord, who hath believed our report?" (Rom. 10:16; Isa. 53:1). "...for with the heart man believeth unto righteousness; and with the mouth confession is made unto salvation. For the scripture saith, Whosoever believeth on him shall not be put to shame. For there is no distinction between Jew and Greek: for the same Lord is Lord of all, and is rich unto all that call upon him: for, Whosoever shall call upon the name of the Lord shall be saved. How then shall they call on him in whom they have not believed? and how shall they believe in him whom they have not heard? and how shall they hear without a preacher? and how shall they preach, except they be sent? even as it is written, How beautiful are the feet of them that bring glad tidings of good things! But they did not all hearken to the glad tidings For Isaiah said, Lord, who hath believed our report? So belief cometh of hearing, and hearing by the word of Christ. But I say, Did they not hear? Yea, verily, Their sound went out into all the earth, and their words unto the ends of the world. But I say, Did Israel not know? First Moses saith, I will provoke you to jealousy with that which is no nation, with a nation void of understanding will I anger you. And Isaiah is very bold, and saith, I was found of them that sought me not; I became manifest unto them that asked not of me. But as to Israel he saith, All the day long did I spread out my hands unto a disobedient and gainsaying people" (Rom. 10:10-21). Moses himself had foreseen that there would be those who were disobedient, and thus he said: "And it shall come to pass, that whosoever will not hearken unto my words which he shall speak in my name, I will require it of him." (Deut. 18:19).

(d) Paul also emphasized that any and all of Israel who would believe would be brought into the covenant (Rom. 11:20-29).

Third, Jeremiah implied that the covenant would be made with those who were willing and not those who were unwilling. He said that God's laws would be put in their inward parts and written on their hearts (Jer. 31:33). It could not be written on the hearts of those who were unwilling. The willingness must be furnished by man. God cannot be willing for us. And thus a Jewish scholar, Yehezkel Kaufmann, wrote; "The prophecy of destruction arose out of the conception of Israel as habitually backsliding from Sinai to the time of Josiah. Experience teaches that mankind as now constituted cannot keep God's covenant, hence a new mankind must be created whose heart God has refashioned, and upon which he has impressed his word as a seal. Jeremiah's prophecy of doom is a vindication of God; his prophecy of consolation is an apology for man. Jeremiah realizes that men cannot fulfill his radical demands without the gracious help of God. What gives this vision its Israelite character is the precondition of repentance. The redeeming act of God waits upon man's initiative; man must take the first step by repenting.[4]

Do not these considerations make it clear that all of Israel did not have to accept the covenant in order for God to abolish the old and to bring in the new? In fact, the psalmist David foresaw that although the people would be in rebellion against Got and His Messiah, that God would establish the Christ as King in spite of their rebellion (Psa. 2).

GENTILES INCLUDED

The prophecy of Moses (Deut, 18:15-19), and of Jeremiah (31:31-34), made no explicit references to the Gentiles. However, other prophecies show that in the days of the Messiah the Gentiles were to be blessed and that the nations throughout the world would be included. In other words, His reign would include Gentiles as well as Jews (Isa. 49:5-7; Acts 13:47). As Paul pointed out: "As he saith also in Hosea, I will call that my people which was not my people; And her beloved, that was not beloved. And it shall be, that in the place where it was said unto them, Ye are not my people, There shall they be called sons of the living God." (Rom. 9:25-26). "But I say, Did Israel not know? First Moses saith, I will provoke you to jealousy with that which is no nation. With a nation void of understanding will I anger you. And Isaiah is very bold, and saith, I was found of them that sought me not; I became manifest unto them that asked not of me. But as to Israel he saith, All the day long did I spread out my hands unto a disobedient and gainsaying people" (Rom 10:19-21).

Yehezkel Kaufmann wrote that "there can hardly be a doubt that the new covenant with Israel has universal significance."[5]

---

[4] Yehezkel Kaufmann, *The Religion of Israel,* University of Chicago Press, 1960, pp. 425-426.

[5] *Ibid,* p. 426.

Since the Messiah was to rule over Gentiles as well as over Jews, it is clear that His rule could not be under the Law of Moses. For the Law of Moses was for a particular nation which was living in a specific land. Even moral duties of the law, such as worshipping of God, and of honoring parents, were tied in with exhortations directed to Israel as a people—and not to the Gentiles. Thus God said: "I am Jehovah thy God, who brought *thee out of the land of Egypt,* out of the house of bondage. Thou shalt have no other gods before me." (Ex. 20:2-3). "Honor thy father and thy mother, that thy days may be long *in the land which Jehovah thy God giveth thee.*" (Ex. 20:12). The keeping of the Sabbath day was tied in with the remembrance that they had been servants in Egypt (Deut. 5:14-15). The old covenant would have to be abolished, since the Gentiles were to be included, because Judaism was in its nature a local and national religion.

A SPIRITUAL PEOPLE

Those with whom the covenant has been made are those both of Jews and of Gentiles who willingly accepted it. Those who accept it become the people of God, the new spiritual Israel. Jewish interpreters agree that the people with a new heart will be a new people. Therefore, as a new people there is neither Jew nor Greek, but a new people with God's law written on their hearts (Heb. 8:10). They are Abraham's seed (Gal. 3:26-29; Rom. 4:1-17), and thus they are the true circumcision (Phil. 3:3-9; Col 2:11-17). They have come unto Mount Zion and the heavenly Jerusalem (Heb. 12:22). This new covenant is not like the old, although it was promised, prophesied and foreshadowed by the old.

NEW COVENANT NECESSITATED A NEW MEDIATOR

The new covenant was not to be like the Mosaic covenant, which was to be abolished. Thus the mediatorship of Moses was to end with the end of his covenant. But if there is to be a new covenant there must be a mediator of that covenant. And what could be more fitting than for that mediator to be the prophet like unto Moses, whose coming Moses prophesied and who was to be the one to whom the people were to listen?

CHRIST DID ESTABLISH A COVENANT

It is a matter of historical fact that Jesus of Nazareth did establish a covenant, and that thousands of Jews as well as of Gentiles accepted it within a few years. None of the prophets of Israel who came after Moses established a covenant. They called people back to the Law of Moses, and this in itself indicated that the prophet like unto Moses had not yet come. A prophet, however, did finally come out of Israel and establish a covenant. Jesus of Nazareth alone, of all those who have arisen in the midst of Israel (Deut. 18:15-19), established a new covenant, a new faith and practice, which has continued to stand even unto this day.

The prophet like unto Moses had to establish a new order of things, for this is implied in the very fact that he would replace Moses. Further, it is taught in Jeremiah's prophecy. It is no objection against this covenant that it is not the old covenant, for Jeremiah said that it would be new and unlike the old (Jer. 31:31-32).

It is also significant that this covenant was established *before,* although only a few years before, *it became impossible for Israel to keep the old covenant.* Around forty years before the destruction of the temple and of Jerusalem in A.D. 70 made it impossible for Israel to keep the old covenant, the covenant of Christ was proclaimed to Israel and thousands accepted it (Acts 2:36-42; Heb. 8:6-13; 12:24; 13:20). Since the old covenant was to be replaced it should be clear that the old was to continue until it was replaced by the new. But the old has long ago ceased to exist, therefore the new which replaced it must have come. And such a covenant was made shortly before it became impossible for Israel to keep the covenant. God, in His providence, abolished even the outward aspects of the covenant, so that Israel could not even keep these. He had already brought in fact the old to an end with the establishment of the new. For around forty years of long-suffering Israel was preached to and the temple stood; and then in A.D. 70 the temple was destroyed and it became impossible to keep the old covenant. However, the gospel covenant is still for all of Israel who will accept it.

CHRIST SUPERSEDED MOSES

The prophet like unto Moses was to take the place of Moses, and thus was to supersede Moses. To be like Moses, and to establish a new covenant, was to replace Moses. That this prophet has come should be evident from the fact that Moses has been superseded and replaced. It is impossible for anyone today to follow Moses and his covenant, and it has been impossible for around two thousand years. It became impossible shortly after Jesus established His covenant. He alone, of all the prophets of Israel, had established a permanent covenant and since then Moses has been superseded.

CHRIST GREATER THAN MOSES

He who superseded Moses would have to be greater than Moses in order to bring Moses' covenant to an end and to establish his own. More people believe in Christ than believed in Moses. Millions know of Moses because they first knew of Christ. In fact, today more people believe that Moses was a prophet of God because they believe in Christ, who said Moses wrote of Him (John 5:46-47), than believe in Moses without believing in Christ. He is greater, for his teaching is greater than that of Moses. It does not have the elaborate ritual, the thousand and one minute regulations, and the localism which Moses' law had. It is a universal religion, but

Moses' covenant was local and national. These things are said not to minimize Moses, for he was a prophet of God. But his work was preparatory and temporary, and according to his own prediction he has given way to the one like unto him; who is in fact greater than Moses. Moses, in effect, taught that he was to be eclipsed, and Christ has eclipsed him. Has not the prophet like unto Moses come? Who else among the descendants of Israel has eclipsed Moses? No one!

NOT LIKE THE OLD

When God said that He would make a new covenant, unlike the old, He did not say that there would not be any points of similarity. There are principles which are rooted in the nature of God, and in the nature which God has given man, and these are found in both covenants.[6] But God through Jeremiah spelled out at least three ways in which the new covenant would be new. In showing in what the newness consisted, it is clear that Jeremiah was not saying that there would not be any points of similarity. For it is obvious that the two covenants would be similar in that both were made by God, under both God had a covenant people, and both were covenants. There would be, however, at least three basic points of dissimilarity. *First,* the law would be in their hearts instead of on tables of stone. *Second,* all would know the Lord. *Third,* their sins and iniquities would be remembered no more (Jer. 31:31-34).

GOD'S LAWS ON THEIR HEARTS

The Lord prophesied that "I will put my laws into their mind, and on their heart also will I write them: and I will be to them a

---

[6] See James D. Bales, Christ The Fulfillment of The Law **and** The **Prophets,** Shreveport, La.: Lambert Book House, 1973. This is the new title under which **Messiah's Mission** has been published.

God, and they shall be to me a people." (Heb. 8:10; Jer. 31:33). It is written on men's hearts through the word of God, for when Jesus sent forth His disciples to bring men into covenant relationship with Him, He told them to make disciples or learners and baptize them into the name of the Father, the Son, and the Holy Spirit. Then they were to be taught to observe all things which Jesus had commanded (Matt. 28:19-20). On Pentecost those who were taught, who received the word and believed, were exhorted to accept Christ (Acts 2:36-41).

The laws being written on the hearts of the covenant people included at least the following. *First,* the inwardness of the new covenant. The old covenant had been written on tables of stone, and it was filled with a multitude of carnal ordinances (Heb. 9:9-10). What a striking contrast there is between the old covenant with its priesthood, its elaborate ritual and ceremony, and the simplicity and inwardness of the new covenant.

Second, a more willing obedience may be indicated since the law would be written on their hearts and minds. We must not assume, however, that there was no obedience from the heart in the Old Testament for God's word was to be stored up in their heart. However, under the new there is a more willing obedience for one is not born into the covenant without the consent of his own will. His mind must be appealed to in order for the law of God to be put into his mind. Therefore, the consent of his will is involved in man's coming into the new covenant. And this attitude must continue in order for one to remain faithful in the covenant.

LAWS

Is law in any sense binding on those who are under the new covenant? Some assume that since we are not under the Old Testament law that the Christian is without law in any sense. If this is true, it is impossible for a Christian to do wrong. Anything that he can possibly do is right for him to do; for there is no law against it. Anything which he does not want to do, it is right for him to refuse to do it, for there is no law which says that he must do it. If there is no law, there can be no transgression, "for every one that doeth sin doeth also lawlessness; and sin is lawlessness." (1 John 3:4). Paul says that through love we fulfill the law. "For this, Thou shalt not commit adultery, Thou shalt not kill, Thou shalt not steal, Thou shalt not covet, and if there be any other commandment, it is summed up in this word, namely, Thou shalt love thy neighbor as thyself. Love worketh no ill to his neighbor: love therefore is the fulfillment of the law" (Rom. 13:9-10). If there is no law for us to fulfill, there is nothing to regulate love. If there is no law which says that love shalt not work ill to thy neighbor, love is under no obligation not to work ill. The golden rule shows that love not only does not work ill, but that love works good to the neighbor (Matt. 7:12). If there is no law which says "Thou shalt", there is no good that we are obligated to work toward our neighbor. Furthermore, if a Christian is not under law in any sense, he is not under the law of love. But what would Christianity be without law and without love? It would not be Christianity.

Laws do apply to Christians. Concerning those baptized, Jesus said, teaching them *to observe all things whatsoever I commanded you*" (Matt. 28:20). Paul wrote: "If any man thinketh himself to be a prophet, or spiritual, let him take knowledge of the things which I write unto you, that they are *the commandment of the Lord*" (1 Cor. 14:37). The church in Jerusalem continued steadfastly in the apostles' doctrine (Acts 2:42). Although Paul was without law, in that he was not under the Law of Moses (and in this sense, too, the Gentiles were without law; although not without law in every sense, Rom. 1:18-32; 2:12-15), yet he said: "not being without law to God, but *under law to Christ...*" (1 Cor. 9:21). He who is under the impression that he is without law in any sense, does not understand the nature of the new covenant, for of it God said: "For this is the covenant that I will make with the house of Israel after those days, saith the Lord; *I will put my laws into their mind,* and *on their heart also will I write them*" (Heb. 8:10). And Moses said that those who did not hearken to the prophet would have it required of them (Deut. 18:19). In other words, men are held accountable as to their treatment of the prophet's word.

It is clear that law in some sense applies to the Christian. It is just as clear that in some sense the Christian is not under law. What is the harmony between these two statements? Paul said that sin should not have dominion over us because we are not under law but under grace (Rom. 6:14). If this meant that law in no sense applies to the Christian, it would mean that we could not sin just because we are not under the law but under grace. Paul would not say in one verse that it is impossible to sin, and then say in the next verse that we should not sin. If we were under law in the sense Paul mentions here, we would be under sin's rulership or dominion. How so? If we had to live a perfect life to be saved, all of us would be under the curse. For the law says that one is cursed unless he does all the law says, and does it all of the time (Gal. 3:10). Having once sinned, sin would be our master and rule over us unto death; if we had to be justified by a law of merit, a law of perfect and perpetual obedience. The Christian is not under law in that he has to earn or merit his salvation. Because of God's grace he can come out from under sin's domination and not reap sin's wages. But under grace he still has laws to follow, and is to yield his body members as instruments of righteousness. But he does not do a perfect job of this. His case would be hopeless if he were to be judged on his merit; if he had to live under law as the standard by which he had to be judged. For not having done it all, and not having done it all the time, he would be under the curse. But forgiveness is available. This grace is not a license to sin, but provides pardon for the penitent sinner (1 John 1:6; 2:4).

ALL KNOW GOD

Jeremiah did not say that everyone in the world will know God; instead, he spoke of those who have entered into covenant relationship with God. He has reference to those with whom the covenant has been made, and on whose hearts God's laws have been written. These will not need to teach their brothers and neighbors, or fellow citizens, in the covenant to know God, for all know Him since they have His law written in their hearts. It does not mean that they shall not need any teaching, but it does show that those in the covenant know God. They were even then being taught in Hebrews. Through the word of the gospel, which had been preached to them and accepted by them, they had come to know God in the saving-relationship in the new covenant (We have dealt with this in some detail in our manuscript on *The New Covenant Is New*).

SINS REMEMBERED NO MORE

God said, through Jeremiah, that "I will be merciful to their iniquities, and their sins will I remember no more." (Heb. 8:12; Jer. 31:34). This implied that under the old covenant sins were remembered in some sense. The Old Testament sacrifices were repeated from time to time. The repetition of the sacrifices showed that the sacrifices were insufficient to really take away sins. On the great Day of Atonement there was a remembrance of sins made again every year (Heb. 10:1-4). Offerings were made for all of Israel's sins (Lev. 16:16, 21). The fact, however, that under the new covenant there would be no more remembrance of sins, indicated that the sacrifice for sin would be sufficient. And indeed it is, for Jesus Christ, as Isaiah prophesied, is our one sufficient sacrifice for sins (Isa. 53; Heb. 10:1-20).

The fact that the sacrifice under the new covenant would be sufficient indicates that the temple system, which was the system wherein the sacrifices for sins were offered continually, would be done away with. The temple in the Old Testament was the place of the Divine presence in a unique sense. But under the new covenant the church itself is a living temple (Eph. 2:20-23), and our bodies are the temple of the Spirit (1 Cor. 6:19-20). With God's laws in our hearts, and His Spirit dwelling within, there is no need for the old temple. Are not the days of the new covenant, insofar as its relationship to the old covenant is concerned, well described by Jeremiah when he said: "they shall say no more, The ark of the covenant of Jehovah; neither shall it come to mind; neither shall they remember it; neither shall they miss it; neither shall it be made any more"? (Jer. 3:16)

Our conclusion is that although there are some similarities between the covenants, the new covenant is unlike the old in the basic features which were set forth in Jeremiah's prophecy. Christ, the Prophet like unto Moses, has established His new covenant just as Moses implied and Jeremiah prophesied.

OBJECTING TO THE FULFILLMENT

One of the objections brought against the first teachers of the gospel was that they preached a message which differed from that of Moses. "And Stephen, full of grace and power, wrought great wonders and signs among the people. But there arose certain of them that were of the synagogue called the synagogue of the Libertines, and of the Cyrenians, and of the Alexandrians, and of them of Cilicia and Asia, disputing with Stephen. And they were not able to withstand the wisdom and the Spirit by which he spake. Then they suborned men, who said, We have heard him speak blasphemous words against Moses, and against God. And they stirred up the people, and the elders, and the scribes, and came upon him, and seized him, and brought him into the council, and set up false witnesses, who said, This man ceaseth not to speak words against this holy place and the law: for we have heard him say, that this Jesus of Nazareth shall destroy this place, and shall change the customs which Moses delivered unto us." (Acts 6:8-14). Stephen had not blasphemed, but it is true that the new covenant did supersede the old; and therefore changed the things which Moses had delivered. But this was not blasphemy unless it can be proved that Jesus was not from God and that He did not have the authority to create the new covenant. Did Moses blaspheme because he indicated that a change would come when the prophet like unto him took his place? Did Jeremiah blaspheme when he said that God would make a new covenant which would be unlike the old? Did Micah blaspheme when he said: "Therefore shall Zion for your sake be plowed as a field, and Jerusalem shall become heaps, and the mountain of the house as the high places of a forest." (Micah 3:12). Whenever these prophecies were fulfilled the temple and the holy city would be destroyed, and the customs delivered by Moses would be changed. And as a matter of fact, Jerusalem was destroyed and the customs delivered by Moses have been changed, and no one today can keep the Law of Moses. Any objections to these things are objections to the fulfillment of prophecies which were uttered by prophets of Israel. They are therefore attacks on the Old Testament itself.

CHAPTER 5

Predictions By Moses

A prophet, as an inspired spokesman for God, did more than predict. However, when God so willed, he did predict. Moses was not only the mediator of the old covenant, but he also made some predictions concerning Israel. Most of these are found in Deuteronomy 28. Moses does not speak in vague terms concerning the waxing and waning of Israel, but gives some specifics which are too detailed to have been based on human foresight. Taken as a whole this series of predictions constitutes a miracle of foreknowledge and gives us reason for accepting the inspiration of Moses.

THE CHOICE WHICH WAS SET BEFORE ISRAEL

Israel's obedience to God would be blessed with blessings both material and spiritual. Worldly prosperity, fruitfulness of the ground and of their animals, and the blessing of children were promised. Spiritually they were to be established *as a holy people unto God* (Deut. 28:1-14). These blessings were contingent upon obedience. They were to hearken diligently unto the voice of Jehovah and "to observe to do all his commandments" which He had commanded them (Deut. 28:2, 1, 9, 14). However, disobedience would be severely punished (Deut. 28:15-68). The decision was left to them. The pronouncements were so definite and clear that they could not fail to understand them. They had seen what God had done in Egypt and thus they knew that He had the power to sustain His promises (Deut. 29:2-9). They had the power of choice, and thus moral responsibility. Life and death was set before them and they were exhorted to choose life through continual obedience to God's word.

The only choice, however, which they had was between life and death and not between life and something else besides destruction and death. They were free to choose but they had to choose one or the other. They could not refuse to make a decision, for decisions are rendered by actions and not only by words. Once they had made the choice and stayed with the choice, they were not free to negate the consequences of that choice. Each course of conduct had its consequences which could not be divorced from the conduct. They could not legislate against, or lightly brush aside, the consequences of disobedience. Here is how Moses put it:

"See, I have set before thee this day life and good, and death and evil; in that I command thee this day to love Jehovah thy God, to walk in his ways, and to keep his commandments and his statutes and his ordinances, that thou mayest live and multiply, and that Jehovah thy God may bless thee in the land whither thou goest in to possess it. But if thy heart turn away, and thou wilt not hear, but shalt be drawn away, and worship other gods, and serve them; I denounce unto you this day, that ye shall surely perish; ye shall not prolong your days in the land, whither thou passest over the Jordan to go in to possess it. I call heaven and earth to witness against you this day, that I have set before thee life and death, the blessing and the curse: therefore choose life, that thou mayest live, thou and thy seed; to love Jehovah thy God, to obey his voice, and to cleave unto him; for he is thy life, and the length of thy days; that thou mayest dwell in the land which Jehovah sware unto thy fathers, to Abraham, to Isaac, and to Jacob, to give them." (Deut. 30:15-20).

VISIBLE RESULTS?

The results of obedience and of disobedience would be visible to the eye of man. As Richard Whately observed, if Moses had "been a false pretender, he would have known that he could not secure the constant *fulfillment* of his promises and threats And his imposture would have been detected, when men found that they were not regularly rewarded and punished according as they obeyed or disobeyed his law. We may be sure, therefore, that a crafty imposter would not have trusted entirely to promises and threats of temporal goods and evils alone. He would, doubtless, have taught the Israelites to look for a state of future retribution also; which was done by the ancient heathen law-givers. Most of these, probably, did not themselves believe in what they taught about Elysium and Tartarus; but they judged it wise to try to make their people believe it, for the sake of keeping them in awe. And they knew that the falsity of their promises and threats respecting *another world* could not be detected by *experience.*

"And Moses, no doubt, would have proceeded in the same manner, had he been a pretender. But he was fully convinced that the Israelites really did live under that miraculous Providence which he described. And their own experience taught them that what he said was true."[1]

TIME?

It should also be pointed out that this series of prophecies does not involve a specific time element nor does it deal with only one case of disobedience. It deals with the general question of obedience and disobedience; *whenever these characterized Israel.* In other words, it is not like the prophecy of Jonah which said that in forty days Nineveh would be destroyed. It was not a series of

---

[1] Richard Whately, Rise, **Progress,** and **Corruptions of Christianity,** p. 98.

prophecies which had to be all fulfilled at one time, since its fulfillment was conditioned on Israel's obedience or disobedience to God. When Israel became disobedient and God's wrath began to be poured out on her, if she repented God would replace wrath with blessings. More than once Israel did go into disobedience, and then turned, and the full measure of God's wrath was not poured out on her. However, if the full measure was necessary in order to bring her to repentance, God would pour out the full measure. But God would bless Israel when she repented (Deut. 30:1-20).

According to certain Jewish authorities, "all these humiliations were fulfilled during the Second Commonwealth, particularly during the destruction of the Second Temple."[2] The Second Temple was built by Zerubbabel after the return from Persia in 537 B.C. While it is true that Israel's disobedience did result in the destruction of the Second Temple, the temple was later rebuilt. This third temple was started by Herod in 19 B. C. and was finished in A.D. 64. The Romans destroyed it in A.D. 70. Around two thousand years have passed, but still no temple functions in Jerusalem. What disobedience took place in the first century which resulted in the destruction of Jerusalem and the scattering of the nation? *Surely these humiliations of Israel which began in the first century, and have lasted so much longer than any other judgments, are related to Israel's relationship with God.* Such judgments were not the fulfillment of the blessings which were promised if Israel obeyed. Instead, they are judgments such as Moses described, which would come on Israel because of her disobedience. There has been in these judgments the fulfillment of Moses' predictions, far beyond anything in the past.

If Jesus is the Christ, the greatest act of disobedience by Israel

---

[2] Joseph Reider, **Deuteronomy With Commentary,** Philadelphia: The Jewish Publication Society of America, 1948, p. 271.

and in which she has persisted, was the rejection of Jesus. Thus we would expect the full measure of God s judgment, as set forth by Moses, to be in connection with this disobedience of Israel. In our examination of the prophecy we shall notice only incidentally the other cases of disobedience and the more limited judgments. What followed their rejection of Jesus is so fully described by Moses that it is very difficult to avoid the conclusion that, as Moses foretold, it is being required of Israel for refusing to accept the prophet like unto Moses (Deut. 18:15-19).

MOSES' PREDICTIONS

Moses prophesied a wide variety of tribulations which would come to Israel. In some of these God would operate through the natural elements, and in others men would be His instruments of judgment. Not only would the people be affected, but also the land in which they lived.

(1) *Many enemies would rise up against Israel* (Deut. 28:25-26) but their utter desolation would be brought about by *a nation which neither they nor their fathers had known*. This enemy was to spare neither the young nor the old. He was to come from afar (28:36). The Assyrians could be said to have come afar (Isa. 5:26; compare Jer. 5:15; Lam. 4:19; 2 Kings 24:15; 25. 6-7). However, since Israel disobeyed more than once, more than once she was attacked by enemies. And Moses' description well fits Rome who was indeed from afar, whom neither the generation of Moses' day nor their fathers had known, whose tongue they did not understand, and who indeed swooped down on them as a bird of prey might do. They showed favor neither to the old nor to the young; as Josephus pointed out in *Wars of the Jews*: "So Vespasian marched to the city Gadara, and took it upon first onset, because he found it destitute of any considerable number of men grown up and fit for war. He came then into it and *slew all the youth, the Romans having no*

mercy on any age whatsoever: and this was done out of the hatred they bore the nation, and because of the iniquity they had been guilty of in the affair of Cestius. He also set fire not only to the city itself, but to all the villas and small cities that were round about it, some of them were quite destitute of inhabitants, and out of some of them he carried the inhabitants as slaves into captivity."[3]

The Jews recognized that the Romans would kill their old men "and their children and wives." (Par. 25). At Jotapata "the Romans, they so well remembered what they had suffered during the siege, that they spared none, nor pitied any, but drove the people down the precipice from the citadel, and slew them as they drove them down..." (Par. 34).

Something of the same slaughter took place at Gamala. "... nor did anyone escape except two women, who were the daughters of Philip, and Philip himself was the son of a certain eminent man called Jacimus, who had been general of king Agrippa's army; and these did therefore escape, because they lay concealed from the rage of the Romans, when the city was taken; for otherwise *they spared not so much as the infants, of which, many were flung down by them* from the citadel." (4.1.10. See also 6.9.2).

(2) **Their cities would be besieged and captured.** "And they shall besiege thee in all thy gates, until thy high and fortified walls come down, wherein thou trustedst, throughout all thy land; and they shall besiege thee in all thy gates throughout all thy land, which Jehovah thy God hath given thee." (Deut. 28:52). The Jews had several walled and well-fortified cities besides Jerusalem. They trusted in these and thought they were invincible. However, as Reider said in his comment on verse 52: "The people should not expect that a land given to them by God cannot be taken away

---

[3] Hereafter when numbers appear after a quotation from Josephus, they refer to Book, chapter, and paragraph, i.e., 3.7.1, for instance.

from them. This hope is as groundless as that placed in the impregnability of the walls of their cities."[4]

(3) *During the time of war and siege the delicate man and woman would eat their own children.* "And thou shalt eat the fruit of thine own body, the flesh of thy sons, and of thy daughters, whom Jehovah thy God hath given thee, *in the siege* and *in the distress* wherewith thine enemies shall distress thee. The *man* that is *tender* among you, and *very delicate,* his eye shall be evil toward his brother, and toward the wife of his bosom, and toward the remnant of his children whom he hath remaining; *so that he will not give to any of them* of the *flesh of his children* whom he shall eat, because he hath nothing left him, in the siege and in the distress wherewith thine enemy shall distress thee in all thy gates. The tender and delicate *woman* among you *who would not adventure to set the sole of her foot upon the ground* for the delicateness and tenderness, her eye shall be evil toward the husband of her bosom, and toward her son, and toward her daughter, and toward her *afterbirth* (margin) that cometh out from between her feet, and toward *her children* whom she shall bear; for she shall eat them for want of all things *secretly,* in the siege and in the distress wherewith thine enemy shall distress thee in thy gates." (Deut. 28:53-57).

Josephus tells us that during the siege of Jerusalem, "It was now a miserable case, and a sight that would justly bring tears into our eyes, how men stood as to their food, while the more powerful had more than enough, and the weaker were lamenting (for want of it). But the famine was too hard for all other passions, and it is destructive to nothing so much as to modesty; for what was otherwise worthy of reverence, was in this case despised; insomuch that children pulled the very morsels that their fathers were eating out of their very mouths; and what was still more to be pitied, *so did the*

---

[4] Reider, Deuteronomy, p. 266.

mothers do as to their infants; and when those that were most dear were perishing under their hands, they were not ashamed to take from them the very last drops that might preserve their lives..." (5.10.3).

"There was a certain woman that dwelt beyond Jordan, her name was Mary; her father was Eleazer, of the village of Bethezob.... She was eminent for her family and her wealth, and had fled away to Jerusalem with the rest of the multitude, and was with them besieged therein at this time." The things she brought with her were taken from her and when she was able to get food others took it. "It was now become impossible for her any way to find any more food, while the *famine* pierced through her very bowels and marrow, when also her passion was fired to a degree beyond the famine itself; nor did she consult with anything but her passion and the necessity she was in. She then attempted a most unnatural thing, and, snatching up her son, who was a *child sucking at her breast,*...she slew her son, and then roasted him, and ate the one half of him and kept the other half by her, *concealed.* Upon this the seditious came in presently, and smelling the horrid scent of this food, they threatened her, and would cut her throat immediately, if she did not show them what food she had gotten ready. She replied, that 'she had saved a very fine portion of it for them;' and withal uncovered what was left of her son." She said to them Do not you pretend to be either more tender than a woman, or more compassionate than a mother; but if you be so scrupulous, and do abominate this my sacrifice, as I have eaten the one half, let the rest be reserved for me also." (6.3.4).

(4) **They were to be plucked off their land**. "And it shall come to pass, that, as Jehovah rejoiced over you to do you good, and to multiply you, so Jehovah will rejoice over you to cause you to perish, and to destroy you; and *ye shall be plucked from off the land whither thou goest in to possess it*" (28:63). Contrary to their will,

they would be removed violently from the land. Israel rebelled against God more than once and more than once she was removed from the land. The Assyrians despoiled Israel, and even brought in foreigners to inhabit the "cities of Samaria instead of the children of Israel." (2 Kings 17:24). "And it was so, because the children of Israel had sinned against Jehovah their God, who brought them up out of the land of Egypt...." (17:7). They suffered a like fate under the Romans. In reply to an unbeliever, Minucius Felix said "that they forsook before they were forsaken, and that they were not, as you impiously say, taken captive with their God, but they were given up by God as deserters from His discipline."[5]

Eusebius tells us that "in the eighteenth year of the reign of Adrian, when the war had reached its heights at the city of Bitthrea, a very strong fortress not very far from Jerusalem, the siege was continued for some time, and the revolters were driven to the last extreme by hunger and famine. The author of their madness had also suffered his just punishment, and the whole nation from that time was totally prohibited, by the decree and commands of Adrian, from even entering the country about Jerusalem, so that they could not behold the soil of their fathers even at a distance. Such is the statement of Aristo, of Pella. The city of the Jews being thus reduced to a state of abandonment for them, and totally stripped of its ancient inhabitants, and also inhabited by strangers; the Roman city which subsequently arose, changing its name, was called Aelia, in honour of the emperor Aelius Adrian..."[6]

(5) *There was to be a dispersion of the children of Israel among the kingdoms of the earth*. They were to go "among all the kingdoms of the earth." (28:25). "And Jehovah will scatter thee

---

[5] "The Octavius of Minucius Felix," *The Ante-Nicene Fathers*, Buffalo: The Christian Literature Publication Co., 1885, Vol. IV, p. 194.

[6] *Ecclesiastical History*, pp 131-132, Grand Rapids, Mich.: Baker Book House, 1962.

among all peoples, from the one end of the earth even unto the other end of the earth..." (28:64). From one end of the earth to another we find the Jew.

(6) **They were to be tossed to and fro among the nations without finding rest.** "Thou shalt be tossed to and fro among all the kingdoms of the earth." (28:25). "And among these nations *shalt thou find no ease,* and there shall be *no rest* for the sole of thy foot; but Jehovah will give thee there a *trembling heart,* and failing of eyes, and *pining of soul;* and *thy life shall hang in doubt before thee;* and thou shalt fear night and day, and shalt have no assurance of thy life. In the morning thou shalt say, Would it were even! and at even thou shalt say, Would it were morning! for the fear of thy heart which thou shalt fear, and for the sight of thine eyes which thou shalt see." (28:65-67). There always seems to be an uneasiness among at least some of the Jews. Often, as Richard Graves long ago pointed out, "Whenever we find them recovering any degree of populousness, tranquility, and respect, we see the transitory gleam is soon obscured by the darkest shades of sorrow."[7]

In numerous cases history shows that their uneasiness has been justified. Not only did they suffer terrible things during the destruction of Jerusalem in A.D. 70, but many times since then have they been dealt with cruelly. Eusebius tells us that during "the eighteenth year of his (Trajan's) reign, and another commotion of the Jews being raised, he destroyed a very great number of them." They were involved in insurrections in Egypt and Cyrene. "...the emperor suspecting that the Jews in Mesopotamia would also make an attack upon those there, ordered Lucius Quietus to clear the province of them, who also led an army against them, and slew a great multitude of them."[8] Eusebius also tells of how Adrian

---

[7] Richard Graves, On the Four Last Books of the Pentateuch, pp. 415-416

[8] Ecclesiastical History, pp. 128-129

crushed a revolt of the Jews in Judea.[9] Persecution arose in Spain in the beginning of the seventh century, and in 1391, and in the fifteenth century Jews were expelled from Spain and Portugal.[10] Our own day has seen the persecution of the Jews. Hitler made scapegoats of them and slaughtered many. Anti-Semitism, although not widespread, is seen even in our own country. It has gone on for decades in the U.S.S.R. Even in Palestine today, the Jews are not at rest.

(7) **They were to be oppressed and robbed.** "Thou shalt not prosper in thy ways; and thou shalt be only oppressed and robbed always, and there shall be none to save thee..." (28:29-34). "And what frequent seizures have been made of their effects in almost all countries? How often have they been fined and fleeced by almost all governments? How often have they been forced to redeem their lives with what is almost as dear as their lives, their treasure? Instances are innumerable. We will only cite an historian of our own, who says that Henry III 'always polled the Jews at every low ebb of his fortunes. One Abraham, who was found delinquent, was forced to pay 700 marks for his redemption. Aaron, another Jew, protested that the king had taken from him at times 30,000 marks of silver, besides 200 marks of gold, which he had presented to the queen. And in like manner he used many others of the Jews.' And when they were banished in the reign of Edward I, their estates were confiscated, and immense sums thereby accrued to the crown."[11] There have been numerous other cases where money was extorted from them or their properties confiscated.[12]

(8) **Their sons and daughters were to be given to another**

---

[9] Ibid., pp. 131-132.

[10] Isaac Landman, Editor, *The Universal Jewish Encyclopedia*, New York: Universal Jewish Encyclopedia Company, Inc., 1939, Vol. I, p 352

[11] Bishop Newton, op. cit., p. 93

[12] The Universal Jewish Encyclopedia, Vol. I p 352

people. "Thy sons and thy daughters shall be given unto another people; and thine eyes shall look, and fail with longing for them all the day: and there shall be nought in the power of thy hand." (Deut. 28:32). There have been times when force was used to "convert" them to "Christianity".[13]

"And in several countries, in Spain and Portugal particularly, their children have been taken from them by order of the government to be educated in the popish religion. The fourth council of Toledo ordered that all their children should be taken from them for fear that they would partake of their errors, and they should be shut up in monasteries, to be instructed in the Christian truths. And when they were banished from Portugal, 'the king,' says Mariana, 'ordered all their children under fourteen years of age to be taken from them and baptized: a practice not at all justifiable.'"[14]

They would not have the power to recover their children and stay the hand of the persecutor. "By an edict of the Portuguese, the children of the Jews were ordered to be carried to the uninhabited islands; and when, by the king's command, they were had to the ships in which they were to be transported, it is incredible, the Jewish historian (Shebet Judah) says, what howlings and lamentations were made by the women; and there were none who pitied them and comforted them, or could help them."[15]

(9) *Their sons and daughters would be led into captivity*. Thou shalt beget sons and daughters, but they shall not be thine; for they shall go into captivity." (28:41). Ten tribes were carried away by Salmaneser, two by Nebuchadnezzar and almost the entire body of them by the Romans.

(10) *Some would be carried to Egypt in ships as slaves.* "And

---

[13] Ibid., Vol. I, p. 352.

[14] Bishop Newton, *On the Prophecies*, p. 94; also see The Jewish Encyclopedia, Vol II, p 484.

[15] John Gill, Commentary, p. 124

the Lord will bring thee into Egypt again with ships by the way whereof I spake unto thee, Thou shalt see it no more again: and there ye shall sell yourselves unto your enemies for bondmen and bondwomen, and no man shall buy you." (Deut. 28:68). Josephus said that: "So this Fronto slew all those that had been seditious and robbers, who were impeached one by another; but of the young men he chose out the tallest and most beautiful, and reserved them for the triumph; and as for the rest of the multitude, that were above seventeen years old, he put them into bonds, and sent them to the *Egyptian* mines. Titus also sent a great number into the provinces, as a present to them that they might be destroyed upon their theatres, by the sword and by the wild beasts; but those that were under seventeen years of age were sold for slaves. Now during the days wherein Fronto was distinguishing these men, there perished, for want of food, eleven thousand; some of whom did not taste any food, through the hatred their guards bore them, and others would not take in any when it was given them." (6.9.2).

Jerome tells that some who were sent into Egypt, after being conquered by Hadrian, perished by shipwreck. As he put it: "Let us read the old histories and traditions of the Lamenting Jews, that in the tent of Abraham (where now, every year, a busy market is held), after the last overthrow (of the Jews) under Hadrian, many thousand men were sold into slavery, and those who could not be sold were carried into Egypt, and as many were destroyed by shipwreck and starvation as were cut down by the slaughter of the heathen. So these victors, the Lord's avengers, did the killing and felt no remorse. They were selling the sheep and saying, 'Blessed be the Lord, we have been made rich'—this is their sentiment. The Jews have failed (?) because of their sins. Therefore we have crushed them, and from their sale price we have been made rich. Nor is it strange," he says, "if the enemy by the right of victors were killing the sheep and were not grieving; were selling and boasting of their crime, when the shepherds themselves and teachers did not spare them, and by their fault the herd was delivered to the wolves."[16]

(11) *So many of them would be offered as slaves that they would not all find buyers* (Deut. 28:68). John Gill said that: "There were such numbers of them to be sold both at Egypt and at Rome, that the sellers of them had but a poor market for them; and it seems not only because of their number, but the ill opinion had of them as servants. Hegesippus says, 'there were many to be sold, but there were few buyers; for the Romans despised the Jews for service, nor were there Jews left to redeem their own.' It is said, that thirty were sold for a penny...."[17] In Schurer we are told that "a Jewish slave was of no more value than a horse."[18]

The statement which Gill attributes to Hegesippus is found in Ambrose, although Dr. W.M. Green said he did not think that it is from Ambrose of Milan. There we read; "And the Romans, now weary of much slaughter, did not refuse to grant clemency, and because of their eagerness to sell captives they were the more ready to spare their lives. Many were offered for sale, but there were few buyers, since the Romans do not care to have Jews as slaves, and there were no Jews surviving to redeem their kindred, since every one congratulated himself on his escape, even without money. And so here and there they would put aside their fear and

---

[16] Jerome Commentary on Zechariah 11:4-5, PL 25, 1500f. Translated for the author by Professor William M. Green who has been at Pepperdine College since his retirement from the University of California in Berkeley. See also Bishop Newton, op. cit, p. 91; Emil Schurer, A History of the Jewish People in the Time of Jesus Christ. Tr. by John McPhearson, Edinburgh, T. & T. Clark, 1898, Division I, Vol II, P. 314. The question mark indicates some uncertainty as to the exact meaning of the word.

[17] John Gill, p. 130.

[18] Schurer, op. cit., p. 314.

surrender, since there were no bandits present, and the Romans were showing clemency."[19]

On Deut. 28:68, Joseph Reider commented: "This is the climax of all humiliations: your reputation will be so bad that your enemies will dread even to buy you as slaves; everybody will shun you as a people accursed of God. According to RMbN and Abravanel, all these humiliations were fulfilled during the Second Commonwealth, particularly during the destruction of the Second Temple."[20]

(12) *Sojourners among them would be raised and they would be lowered.* "The sojourner (stranger) that is in the midst of thee shall mount up above thee higher and higher; and thou shalt come down lower and lower." (28:43). For centuries after the destruction of Jerusalem, the Jews were in the state of humiliation in Palestine. Even today those in Palestine have not found rest.

(13) *They were to become reduced in number.* "And ye shall be left few in number, whereas ye were as the stars of heaven for multitude; because thou didst not hearken unto the voice of Jehovah thy God." (28:62). Their number was reduced by the wars with the Romans. Josephus said that "now of those that perished by famine in the city, the number was prodigious" (6.3.3). "Now the number of those that were carried captive during this whole war was collected to be ninety-seven thousand: as was the number of those that perished during the whole siege eleven-hundred thousand..." (6.9.3).

"The whole multitude of Jews that were destroyed during the entire seven years before this time, in all the countries of and bordering on Judea, is summed up by Archbishop Usher from Lipsius, out of Josephus, at the Year of Christ 70, and amounts to

---

[19] Ambrose, History of the Fall of the City of Jerusalem, p. 5, 47 (PL 15, 2196) Translated by Dr. William M. Green.

[20] *Deuteronomy*, p. 271.

1,337,490."[21]

(14) *If they turned aside from serving God, they would have to serve their enemies*. "Because thou servest not Jehovah thy God with joyfulness, and with gladness of heart, by reason of the abundance of all things; therefore shalt thou serve thine enemies that Jehovah shall send against thee, in hunger, and in thirst, and in nakedness, and in want of all things: and he shall put a yoke of iron upon thy neck, until he have destroyed thee." (Deut. 28:47-48).

*(15) They were to serve other gods—idols of wood and stone. Jehovah will bring thee, and thy king whom thou shalt set over thee, unto a nation that thou hast not known, thou nor thy fa*thers; and there shalt thou serve other gods, wood and stone." (28:36; Cf. 28:64). This "they were obliged to do in Babylon..."[22] "Without doubt the Israelites in general, who were carried captives by the Assyrians, and many of the Jews in Chaldea, were finally incorporated with the nations among whom they lived, and were given up to their idolatry."[23]

This may also include their bowing down to the images of Roman Catholicism in times past. Long ago John Gill wrote: "Now in Popish countries the Jews have often been prevailed upon to change, or at least dissemble their religion, and embrace Popery; and have worshipped images of wood and stone. The author of the history of their calamities and sufferings owns this: 'multitudes (he says, Shebet Judah, p. 108) in Spain and Portugal forsook the Law of Moses, and joined the Papists, pretending at least to be of their religion.' He makes mention of 16,000 at one time, and some, he says, 'that were driven out of Spain, came into Italy, where the young men pressed with famine could not bear it, and changed

---

[21] Josephus, *The Wars of the Jews*, p. 6. 9. 3. Footnote by William Whiston.

[22] John Gill, op. cit., p. 124.

[23] Scott's Bible, on Deut. 28:36.

their religion, and began to worship images that they might have to satisfy their hunger; and the Papists used to go about with a crucifix in one hand, and a piece of bread in the other, promising the bread to those that would worship the crucifix; and so many famishing persons forsook the Law of Moses, and mixed with them..."[24]

"Basnage said that the 'Spanish and Portugal inquisitions reduce them to the dilemma of being either hypocrites or burnt. The number of these dissemblers is very considerable; and it ought not to be concluded that there are no Jews in Spain or Portugal, because they are not known: They are so much more dangerous, for not only being very numerous, but confounded with the ecclesiastics, and entering into all ecclesiastical dignities.'" (7.33.14).[25]

Reider commented that: "The sojourn in foreign countries inevitably leads to the adoption of foreign gods, either through coercion or the strong impulse of imitation."[26]

The Jewish Encyclopedia records centuries of persecution in Spain. Sisebut decreed that all Jews must be baptized or leave. Some left but the greater number embraced Catholicism outwardly. The Fourth Toledan Council "ordered that the children of" Jews "should be taken from their parents and given to Christians" to be educated. Property was confiscated during the reign of some rulers. In 1250, for the Jews to proselyte Gentiles resulted in death and

---

[24] John Gill, op. cit., p. 129.

[25] Quoted by Newton, *op. cit.*, p. 95. See also Yitzhak Baer, *A History of the Jews in Christian Spain*, Philadelphia: Jewish Publication Society, 1966, including p. 492.

[26] *Deuteronomy*, p. 262. For examples of persecution by the Romans, see Emil Shurer, *A History of the Jewish People in the Time of Jesus Christ*, New York: Charles Scribner's Sons, First Division, Vol. II, and Max L. Marggoles and Alexander Marx, Philadelphia: The Jewish Publication Society of America, 1927.

confiscation of property. They could not associate with Christians, and had to wear a badge unless the king exempted someone.[27]

(16) ***They would be smitten with madness at times because of some of the persecutions***. "Jehovah will smite thee with madness." (Deut. 28:28). "So that thou shalt be mad for the sight of thine eyes which thou shalt see." (28:34). Josephus records some examples of the madness to which they were driven by their oppressions. Men chose to slay their own families and lots were drawn to see who would slay them. The last one killed himself (Book 7, Chapters 6, 8 and 9).

"But for Caesar, he excused himself before God as to this matter, and said, that he had proposed peace and liberty to the Jews, as well as an oblivion of all their former insolent practices; but that they, instead of concord, had chosen sedition; instead of peace, war; and before satiety and abundance, a famine That they had begun with their own hands to burn down that temple which we have preserved hitherto; and that therefore they deserved to each such food as this was." (6.3.5).

When Gamala was taken, men threw their wives and children down precipices. "But so it happened, that the anger of the Romans appeared not to be so extravagant as *was the madness of those* that were now taken, while the Romans slew but four thousand, whereas the number of those that had thrown themselves down, was found to be five thousand," (4.1.10)

The Jews within Jerusalem fought even among themselves. "There were besides disorders and civil wars in every city and all those that were at quiet from the Romans turned their hands one against another. There were also bitter contest between those that were fond of war, and those that were desirous of peace. At the first this quarrelsome temper caught hold of private families, who

---

[27] The Jewish Encyclopedia, Vol. II, pages 484, 289.

could not agree among themselves; after which those people that were the dearest to one another broke through all restraints with regard to each other, and every one associated with those of his own opinion and began already to stand in opposition to one another; so that seditions arose every where... And in the first place, all the people of every place betook themselves to rapine; after which they got together in bodies, in order to rob the people of the country, insomuch that for barbarity and iniquity those of the same nation did no way differ from the Romans; nay, it seemed to be a much lighter thing to be ruined by the Romans than by themselves." (4.3.2).

In another place he again refers to the "sedition" which arose between the people of the city of Jerusalem (1.7.2). He has this to say with reference to one of them. "But for the present sedition one should not mistake if he called it a sedition begotten by another sedition, and *to be like a wild* beast *grown mad,* which, for want of food from abroad, fell now upon eating its own flesh." (5.1.1).

(17) *The* **land was** *to* **then** *get* **its** *Sabbath* **rest**. God said that He would make their cities waste. "And I will bring the land into desolation; and your enemies that dwell therein shall be astonished at it... Then shall the land enjoy its Sabbaths, as long as it lieth desolate, and ye are in your enemies' land; even then shall the land rest, and enjoy its Sabbaths. As long as it lieth desolate it shall have rest, even the rest which it had not in your Sabbaths, when ye dwelt upon it." (Lev. 26:31-35). They were supposed to leave the land uncultivated every seventh year (Lev. 25:1-22). Often they failed to do this. When they were rooted up out of the land it would be left desolate and untilled. This would be the way in which it got its Sabbath rests. For example, Zedekiah did "that which was evil in the sight of Jehovah...they [the people, J.D.B.] mocked the messengers of God, and despised his words, and scoffed at his prophets, until the wrath of Jehovah arose against his people, till there

was no remedy."

"Therefore he brought upon them the king of the Chaldeans... And them that had escaped from the sword carried he away to Babylon; and they were servants to him and his sons until the reign of the kingdom of Persia: to fulfill the word of Jehovah by the mouth of Jeremiah, until the land had enjoyed its Sabbaths: for as long as it lay desolate it kept Sabbath, to fulfill threescore and ten years." (2 Chron. 36:12, 16-21).

(18) *They* **were not** *to* **perish entirely**. They were to continue to exist as a distinct people. Moses said these curses, if they did not obey God and if they did not turn to Him (Deut. 28:45; 30:1-3), would "be upon thee for a sign and for a wonder, and upon thy seed for ever." (28:46, 62). In spite of all their adversities, in spite of the fact that some people contemporary with ancient Israel have long ago ceased to exist, the Jew is still with us. More than once he has stood by the grave of his oppressor.

(19) *They* **would become** *a* **hiss and a byword.** "And thou shalt become an astonishment, a proverb, a byword, among all the peoples whither Jehovah shall lead thee away." (Deut. 28:37). They were to be viewed with amazement and horror, to be a by-word and to be the object of taunts or sharp cutting words. As Reider observed, they were to be "an object of gibes and quips on the part of your enemies who contemplate your unexampled fall into disgrace."[28] And so it has been. "The Jew was a stock figure for ridicule on the comic stage, and the poets from Horace to Juvenal made him the butt of their satire."[29] John Gill tells us that in his day, the 18th century, in England, it was common to say: "Do you think I am a Jew?" "None but a Jew would have done such a thing." William H. Thomson, missionary in Palestine in the 19th

---

[28] Deuteronomy, page 262.

[29] Joseph Berhard, The Vatican as a World Power, p. 3.

century told of a plague in Sidon during which a "native Christian" asked a Moslem how many persons had died in that city that day. "Seven men and one Jew!" "This was the characteristic answer."

"The disgrace of defeat has sometimes clung to a race for generations, especially when religious differences have increased the arrogance of the conquerors, as among the Mohammedans; but the universality and persistence of the opprobrium attached to the Jew throughout the world is wholly without its counterpart, and constitutes not the least singular aspect of this strange subject. The Jew, indeed, is the only universal human proverb."[30] Count Heinrich Coudenhove-Kalergi has presented in summary form some of the bywords and taunts which have been uttered concerning Jews. Of them it has been said: "The Jews! expel them! no, kill them! no baptize and convert them! no, specific laws will suffice. Thus, for centuries, the cry of the Anti-Semite has resounded in its fourfold nuance in all kingdoms and in all countries, republics not excepted. The reasons invoked are very well known.

"They are deicides, stubborn and stiffnecked; they do not understand their own Hebrew Bible, are faithless and mutilate many texts of Holy Writ, distorting their clear meaning and sense; they are usurers and pimps; their Talmud permits them to kill the non-Jews, to cheat and deceive them, to ruin them by extortion and usury, to forswear themselves to the detriment of Christians if it be done to the advantage of a Jew; they consider themselves alone as men, while the Christians are cattle and worshippers of idols. They crucify and slaughter little children and use their blood for the preparation of their unleavened bread and for other purposes; in their writings Christ, the Holy Virgin and the Church, are being abused; they desecrate and mutilate Holy Hosts which begin to bleed, and are responsible for the immorality of our times; in their

---

[30] William M. Thompson, *The Great Argument*, p. 155.

newspapers and in other productions of their press they corrupt Christian morals, they ruin simple-minded peasants, officers, the commercial and industrial classes and honest artisans, by their usury; they lower the prices of commodities and wages; they bribe kings, emperors, cabinet-ministers, parliamentarians and judges; they seduce chaste maidens and married women, and thanks to their cunning and crafty financial operations, they have lured into their nets all governments; they influence the cabinets of the states and are the leaders of freemasonry and of social democracy; they poisoned the wells and by means of witchcraft brought about devastating epidemics; they worship the golden head of an ass, and they annually fattened and slaughtered a Greek; they kill and poison prophets; they are rapacious culture; Bedouins, unscrupulous, cruel, sensual and blood-thirsty; they hate the whole world and do not believe one word of what the Church is teaching; even the uncreated holy Koran they consider to be a worthless compilation; Christ, they say, is a magician, and Mohammed an imposter.

"Indeed it is a long record!

"I confess that I, too, have repeatedly heard most of the above quoted accusations, had at one time believed them and had even come so far as to pray with the Anti-Semites: 'Oh Lord, send us again Moses so that he might lead his brethren by race to the Holy land. Divide the sea once more and let the two pillars of water stand like a wall of rock. And when the entire people of the Jews will once more have entered these watergroves, then, oh Lord, shut the door so that we poor Christians might at least have peace and rest.'"[31]

One is not being anti-Semitic in pointing to these fulfillments

---

[31] Count Heinrich Coudenhove-Kalergi. Edited and brought up to date by Count Richard Coudenhove-Kalergi. Authorized English transition by Dr. Angelo S. Rappaport, *Anti-Semitism Throughout the Ages*, Hutcheson and Co., Ltd. London, 1935, pp. 23-24.

of Moses' prophecy. If to point to the fulfillment is anti-Semitic, Moses was anti-Semitic in prophesying these things and Jewish commentaries are anti-Semitic for commenting on Deut. 28. The attitude of the Christian should be one of good will. It is the author's conviction that good will is being manifested in calling attention to the reasons for our conviction that Christ is the prophet like unto Moses; and that because of the rejection of Christ it has been required of Israel, as Moses foretold, for many centuries.

(20) *Gods judgments on them would be used as a sign and a wonder.* "And they shall be upon thee for a sign and for a wonder, and upon thy seed for ever. Because thou servedst not the Lord thy God with joyfulness, and with gladness of heart, for the abundance of all things" (Deut. 28:40-47). Such terms as *signs* and *wonders* were used to refer to God's miracles in connection with His deliverance of Israel from Egypt.[32] Moses' prophecy of the coming judgments on Israel constitutes a miracle of foreknowledge. In this very book we are using these things as a sign which signified that God indeed spoke through Moses. As William M. Thomson said: "Is it not time to ponder the meaning of a testimony like this, the testimony" of centuries?[33] For it is not a matter of opinion but a matter of fact that the Jewish nation has actually suffered the things which Moses prophesied.

GUESSES?

Infidels cannot overthrow these prophecies by saying that other peoples have been persecuted. Where is there a parallel to the history of Israel, in any of the following features? *First,* their history was prophesied long before these things took place. *Second,* their continued existence. *Third,* the minute details of the prophecy.

---

[32] Reider, *Deuteronomy*, pp. 57, 265.

[33] Thomson, The Great Argument, p 157

A century ago Richard Whately well pointed out "That these prophecies are such as no one would ever have made by *guess*. Nothing could have been more unlikely than the events which have befallen the Jewish nation. Nothing like them has ever been fore-told of any other nation, or has ever happened to any other. There are, indeed, many cases recorded in history of one nation conquer-ing another, and either driving them out of the country or keeping them in subjection. But in all these cases the conquered people who have lost their country either settle themselves in some other land, or, if they are wholly dispersed generally become gradually mixed and blended with other nations; as for example, the Britons and Saxons, the Danes and Normans, have been mixed up into one people in England.

"The only people who at all resemble the Jews, in having been widely dispersed and yet remaining distinct, are those commonly called Gypsies, and whose proper name is Zinganies, or Jingames... And they are widely scattered through the world, keep-ing up their language, and some customs of their own, in all the countries through which they wander. They are certainly a very remarkable people; and if there had been any prophecy (which there was not) of their being thus dispersed, we might well have believed that such a prophecy must have come from inspiration.

"But in some remarkable points their condition differs from that of the Jews, and is less unaccountable. First, they do not (like the Jews) live in towns among other men, and in houses; but dwell in tents, by the roadsides and on commons, leading the life of strolling tinkers, peddlers and fortune-tellers. This roaming life, of course, tends to keep them separate from the people of the coun-tries in which they are found.

"But, secondly, the chief difference is, that the Gypsies are al-ways ready, when required, to profess the religion of the country, whether Christian or Mohammedan, or any other; seeming to have no religion of their own, and to be quite indifferent on the subject. The Jews, on the contrary, always, when they are allowed, settle in towns along with other men; and are kept distinct from them by their religion, and by nothing else. They are the only people who are everywhere separated from the people of the country in which they live, entirely by their peculiar faith and religious observances; and *that* too though their religion is such (which is the strongest point of all) that the most important part of its ordinances—the sacrifices ordained in their law—cannot be observed by them.

"The Jews, therefore, in their present condition, are a kind of standing miracle; being a monument of the wonderful fulfillment of the most extraordinary prophecies that were ever delivered; which prophecies they themselves preserve and bare witness to, though they shut their eyes to the fulfillment of them. No other account than this of the present state and past history of the Jews ever has been or can be given, that is not open to objections greater than all the objections put together that have ever been brought against Christianity."[34]

NATURAL LAW?

These prophecies were uttered long before the event and were not based upon natural causes or principles which would work to the undoing of the Jews. They were not based upon history, upon observation, but upon inspiration.

"It is obvious to remark, how entirely unconnected are such blessings as security from warlike enemies, and the enjoyment of rain from heaven, with the observance of a religious code (Deut. 28); and how idle and unmeaning such promises would have appeared, to any people not deeply impressed, by immediate and

---

[34] Whately, Lessons on Morals, and Christian Evidence, Cambridge: John Bartlett, 1856, pp. 297-300.

clear experience, with the conviction that a supernatural power dictated, and would certainly execute, the promises thus held out. The sacred history records the enjoyment of such prosperity as is thus predicted, during that period of the Jewish state when the divine law was most zealously observed, the latter part of the reign of David, and the entire reign of Solomon."[35]

"The Jewish Lawgiver refers not to political causes [for their persecutions and dispersions, J.D.B.]. He does not tell his countrymen that if they violate his agrarian[36] law, they would overturn the balance of their government; that if they do not preserve their military enrollments, they cannot resist the attacks of their enemies. He does not warn them, that if they neglect agriculture and commerce they would sink into poverty, or be exposed to famine. He does not exhort them to observe the progress of their neighbors in the art of war, and adopt their improvements. He does not caution them to study the subtleties of policy, and to cultivate the friendship of some of the adjoining states as a protection against the ambition of others. He displays no anxiety to rouse in them a spirit of military glory in order to secure them from invasion, or to refine them by literary pursuits in order to exalt their character. His cautions, his warnings, his counsels, are all directed *to this single point*—their *obedience to the Great Jehovah (*Deut. 28:58). Now it is remarkable, in this view of the subject, that many particulars of this law were, according to the usual maxims of human wisdom, directly hostile to the temporal greatness of the people. All the particularities of their ritual, of their peculiar food, of their singular customs, tended to exclude or to offend strangers, and thus impede commerce. They were forbidden to multiply horses (Deut. 17:16); and thus deprived of cavalry and chariots, a species of force so im-

---

[35] Graves, On the Pentateuch, pp. 404-405.

[36] Property-related laws.

81

portant. The assembly of all their adult males three times in the year at a place where the Lord chose to place his Name, necessarily left their frontiers as often exposed to every invader. And against this obvious and imminent danger their Lawgiver held them no security, but this assurance of their God (Exod. 34:24). Thus also the observance of the sabbatical year, which required them to leave their lands untilled every seventh year, seemed to expose them as often to the attacks of famine; against which their Lawgiver held out no security but the assurance of the same God (Lev 25:21). No man will assert that any mere human sagacity could foresee that the neglect of either of these last precepts had naturally any tendency to hasten the ruin of the Jewish state, or prolong the captivity of the Jewish people." (Cf, Lev. 26:32-35).[37]

Although the prophecies were not based on natural laws, it is true that some of the consequences of Israel's disobedience were based on the working of moral and spiritual laws. Long ago Jeremiah warned that in certain matters God would bring evil upon a people, *even the fruit of their own thought* (Jer. 6:19). Some of the attitudes and positions which led Israel to reject Christ have resulted in some of the opposition which she has received from others. For example, Israel in Jesus' day was determined that the Messiah must set up an earthly kingdom which would exalt the nation of Israel. Christ proclaimed a spiritual kingdom. Some wanted to take Him and by force make Him king (John 6:15), but He refused such a kingdom. This same conviction, that God's kingdom must be an earthly state and nation, was a powerful factor in their revolt against Rome and the destruction of Jerusalem by Rome.

GOD OF MERCY

That God is the God of mercy is not an indictment against this

---

[37] Ibid., 409-411.

chapter. God had *dealt graciously* with them. He had blessed them and promised them future blessings if they continued within the covenant. But *they were warned* that these things would come upon them if they forsook the covenant (Deut. 29:25-29). The terrible picture which is painted by Moses, in contrast with the beautiful picture of the life of obedience, should have served as a *sufficient warning* to them. Out of mercy this warning was given that they might not go into disobedience. The chastisements which have come upon them were also for the *purpose of awakening them* that they may seek for the cause of their troubles and find that they have come as a result of forsaking the covenant and rejecting the Son of God. Then, too, Moses said *God would bless them whenever they return to Him.* "And it shall come to pass, when all these things are come upon thee, the blessing and the curse, which I have set before thee, and thou shalt call them to mind among all the nations, whither Jehovah thy God hath driven thee, and shalt return unto Jehovah thy God, and shalt obey his voice according to all that I command thee this day, thou and thy children, with all thy heart, and with all thy soul; that then Jehovah thy God will turn thy captivity, and have compassion upon thee, and will return and gather thee from all the peoples, whither Jehovah thy God hath scattered thee. If any of thine outcasts be in the uttermost parts of heaven, from thence will Jehovah thy God gather thee, and from thence will he fetch thee; and Jehovah thy God will bring thee into the land which thy fathers possessed, and thou shalt possess it; and he will do thee good, and multiply thee above thy fathers. And Jehovah thy God will circumcise thy heart, and the heart of thy seed, to love Jehovah thy God with all thy heart, and with all thy soul, that thou mayest live. And Jehovah thy God will put all these curses upon thine enemies, and on them that hate thee, that persecuted thee. And thou shalt return and obey the voice of Jehovah, and do all his commandments which I command thee this day. And Jehovah thy God will make thee plenteous in all the work of thy hand, in the fruit of thy body, in the fruit of thy cattle, and in the fruit of thy ground, for good: for Jehovah will again rejoice over thee for good, as he rejoiced over thy fathers; if thou shalt obey the voice of Jehovah thy God, to keep his commandments and his statutes which are written in this book of the law; if thou turn unto Jehovah thy God with all thy heart, and with all thy soul.

For this commandment which I command thee this day, it is not too hard for thee, neither is it far off. It is not in heaven, that thou shouldest say, Who shall go up for us to heaven and bring it unto us, and make us to hear it, that we may do it? Neither is it beyond the sea, that thou shouldest say, Who shall go over the sea for us, and bring it unto us, and make us to hear it, that we may do it? But the word is very nigh unto thee, in thy mouth, and in thy heart, that thou mayest do it." (Deut 30:1-15). Under the gospel age the blessings are basically spiritual!

LESSONS

From this prophecy of Moses we can learn several things:

First, God's face is set against sin. It is not a light matter to live in disobedience to the will of God. Since God *is,* since man is His creature, since God has revealed His will to man, and since man is an accountable being, the most serious matter in the world is our relationship to God.

Second, Moses spoke by inspiration of God. His predictions concerning Israel are too minute to be the result of human insight.

Third, through these judgments God is trying to tell Israel that she has been living in disobedience to Him. If Israel had been living in *obedience* to God for the past two thousand years, she would have been living under the blessings of God which Moses predicted in Deuteronomy 28 for Israel. However, she has been living for two thousand years under the curses which Moses set forth as her lot if she lived in disobedience. Moses further said that, when the prophet like unto him came, if they did not hearken to Him, God would require it of them (Deut. 18:18-19). Not many years before the destruction of Jerusalem in AD 70 Israel rejected Jesus of Nazareth. Jesus warned them in a parable of the judgment to which they were subjecting themselves (Mt. 21:33-46).

To repeat an earlier quotation, Minucius Felix pointed out around 210 A.D., "...That they forsook before they were forsaken, and that they were not, as you impiously say, taken captive with their God, but they were given up by God as deserters from His discipline."[38]

Richard Whately well observed that: "One of the most remarkable points relative to these predictions respecting the Jews, and their present condition, is this: that the judgments spoken of by Moses were threatened in case of their departing from the law which he delivered, and especially in case of their worshipping false gods; and yet, though in former times they were so apt to fall into idolatry, they have always, since the destruction of Jerusalem, steadily kept clear of that sin; and have professed to be most scrupulous observers of the law of Moses. And what is more, all the indignities and persecutions that any of them are exposed to, appear to be the *consequence* of their keeping to their religion, and not of their forsaking it. For a Jew has only to give up his religion, and conform to that of the country he lives in, whether Christian, Mohammedan, or Pagan, and lay aside the observances of the law of Moses, and he immediately ceases to be reproached as a Jew and an alien, and is mingled with the people around him. So that the Jews of the present day seem to be suffering, for their observance of the law, just the penalties threatened for their *depar-*

---

[38] "The Octavius of Minucius Felix." *The Ante-Nicene Fathers,* Buffalo, N. Y.; The Christian Literature Publishing Co., 1885m Vol IV, p. 194

ture from it.

"At first sight, this seems very hard to explain; but, on reflection, you will find the difficulty cleared up, in such a way as to afford a strong confirmation of your faith. First, you should observe, that the Jews themselves admit that a Christ or Messiah was promised them; and that to reject Him on his coming would be an act of rebellion against the Lord their God. Moses foretold that the Lord should raise up from among them a Prophet like Moses himself; and 'whosoever should not hear that Prophet,' God 'would require it of him'; and 'that he should be destroyed from among the people.' (Deut. 18:15-19; Acts 3:22, 23). This is generally understood (as it is applied in the Acts) to relate to the Messiah or Christ; whom the other prophetical writers of the Old Testament (as both Christians and Jews are agreed) more particularly foretold and described. Now we hold that the Jews have been guilty of this very act of disobedience in rejecting the Christ. And though they, of course, do not confess themselves thus guilty, because they deny that Jesus of Nazareth was the true Christ, yet they so far agree with us as to knowledge, that the rejecting of the true Christ on his coming would be such a sin as would expose them to the judgments which Moses threatened.

"To us, therefore, who do believe in Jesus, this affords an explanation of their suffering these judgments. But, secondly, besides this, you will perceive, on looking more closely, that the Jews of these days do *not* really observe the law of Moses, though they profess and intend to do so. They have, indeed, kept to the *faith* [to certain of their convictions J.D.B.] of their forefathers; but not to their religious *observances.* For the chief part of the Jewish worship consisted of offering sacrifices distinctly appointed by the Lord himself, in the law delivered by Moses. There was a sacrifice appointed to be offered up every day, and two on the Sabbath; besides several other sacrifices on particular occasions. Now, the modern Jews, though they abstain from certain meats forbidden in their law, and observe strictly the Sabbath and several other ordinances, yet do not offer any sacrifices at all; though sacrifices were appointed as the chief part of their worship.

"The reason of this is that they were strictly forbidden to offer sacrifices except in the *one place* which should be appointed by the Lord for that purpose. And the place last fixed on for these offerings having been the Temple at Jerusalem, which was destroyed about seventeen hundred years ago, and has never been restored, the Jews are now left without any place in which they can lawfully offer the sacrifices which their law enjoins.

"The Jews, accordingly, of the present day, plead that it is not from willful disobedience that they neglect these ordinances but because they cannot help it. But to say that it is not their own fault that they do *not* observe the ordinances of their religion, is quite a different thing from saying that they do observe them. They may explain w*hy* they cannot keep the Law of Moses; but they cannot say that they do keep it.

"Now Christians hold that the ceremonies of that law were not originally designed to be observed by all nations, and for ever; that 'the law had only a shadow of good things to come' (Heb. 10:1), that is, of the Gospel; and that it was designed that the sacrificing of lambs and bullocks should cease at the coming of the Christ [And the establishment of His covenant. J.D.B.]. A Jew, on the contrary, will not allow that these were designed ever to cease; but he cannot deny that they *have* ceased and that for above seventeen centuries. Let a Jew explain, if he can, how it is that for so long a time Providence has put it out of the power of the Jews to observe the principal part of their religion which they maintain was intended to be observed forever.

"And this also is very remarkable, that the religion of the Jews is almost the only one that *could* have been abolished *against the will* of the people themselves, and while they resolved firmly to maintain it. *Their* religion, and theirs only, could be, and has been, thus abolished in spite of their firm attachment to it, on account of its being dependent on a particular *place*—the Temple at Jerusalem, The Christian religion, or, again, any of the Pagan religions, could not be abolished by any force of enemies, if the persons professing the religion were sincere and resolute in keeping to it."

"But it was not so with the Jews. Their religion was so framed as to make the observance of its ordinances impossible when their Temple was finally destroyed. It seems to have been designed and contrived by Divine Providence, that, as their *law* was to be brought to an end by the Gospel (for which it was a preparation), so all men were to *perceive* that it did come to an end, notwithstanding the obstinate rejection of the Gospel by the greater part of the Jews. It was not left to be a question, and a matter of *opinion,* whether the sacrifices instituted by Moses were to be continued or not; but things were so ordered as to put it out of man's power to continue them."[39]

A new covenant has been established, and the judgments predicted by Moses have come upon Israel. Is not the Messiah here, and has not Israel sinned in rejecting Him?

Fourth, Christians must recognize that they must walk in obedience or they will come under the judgment of God. As Paul warned the Romans: "Thou wilt say then, Branches were broken off, that I might be grafted in. Well; by their unbelief they were broken off, and thou standest by thy faith. Be not high-minded, but fear: for if God spared not the natural branches, neither will he spare thee. Behold then the goodness and severity of God: toward them that fell, severity; but toward thee, God's goodness, if thou continue in his goodness: otherwise thou also shalt be cut off. And

---

[39] Whately, *op. cit.,* pages 293-296.

they also, if they continue not in their unbelief, shall be grafted in: for God is able to graft them in again." (Rom. 11:19-23).

CHAPTER 6

Predictions By Christ

Christ bore witness to Himself by the miracles which He performed while on earth, the words which He spoke, the prophecies which He uttered and the moral transformations which He has wrought since His day. We shall consider His prophecies. Those whose fulfillment is recorded in the New Testament will not carry as much weight with the unbeliever as those whose fulfillment is found in later times. But even those fulfilled during the lifetime of the apostles ought to be given fair consideration as it is extremely unlikely that the men who wrote the New Testament would be guilty of "pious fraud." They maintained that these were uttered prior to their fulfillment. Then, too, the fulfillment of certain prophecies after the close of the New Testament confirms those within it.

In working His miracles Christ appealed to eye-witnesses and said that His works bore witness of Him. In making predictions He appealed to subsequent history and said that He had told them before it came to pass "that, when it is come to pass, ye may believe that I am he." (John 13:19).

PREDICTIONS WHOSE FULFILLMENTS ARE FOUND WITHIN THE NEW TESTAMENT

1. Jesus told His disciples where they would find a colt whose master would allow them to take it to Christ. It was just as He had said it would be (Mark 11:2-7).

2. Jesus said that in the city they would meet a man bearing a pitcher of water and that when they followed him to his place of abode they would find an upper room furnished and there Christ would observe the Passover. They found it so (Mark 14:13-16).

3. Christ predicted His betrayal (Matt. 20:18).

4. Jesus said that <u>one</u> of His disciples would betray him (Matt. 26:21; Mark 14:18). One did.

5. He indicated that Judas would do it (John 13:26). Judas betrayed Him for thirty pieces of silver (Matt. 26:14-16 47-49).

6. Jesus said that His disciples would flee in the time of danger (Mark 14:27; Matt. 26:31). This they did even unto the last man (John 18:8-9, 15-18, 25-27; Matt. 26:56),

7. In spite of his boasting Peter's denial was foretold. Before the cock crew twice Peter denied him thrice (Mark 14:30; Luke 22:60-62).

8. Jesus said that He would suffer many things (Matt. 16:21). He suffered anguish in anticipation of the cross, He suffered the desertion of His disciples. He suffered rejection and persecution, (Matt. 26:4, 36-46, 66; 27:26; John 19:18).

9. Jesus said that He was to suffer in Jerusalem (Matt. 16:21; Luke 24:18). And it was in Jerusalem, around which so many sacred memories cluster, that the sinless One was raised upon a cross.

10. Jesus said that He would suffer at the hands of the chief priests (Mark 10:33; Matt. 16:21; 26:3-4; 27:2).

11. Jesus said that He would be mocked, and mockery was one of the cruelties which he had to suffer (Mark 9:12; Luke 18:32; Matt. 26:67-68; 27:27, 31, 39-44; Luke 23:11).

12. Jesus foretold His death by crucifixion (John 3:14; 8:28; 12:32-33; Matt. 20:19; 27:31; Luke 23:33; Mark 15:20, 25).

13. Jesus predicted that He would be mocked, scourged, and spit upon by Gentiles. The chief priests would deliver "Him unto the Gentiles: and they shall mock him, and shall spit upon him..." (Mark 10:33-34; Luke 18:31-33). At the palace of the high priest He was buffeted, smitten, and spit upon (Matt. 26:67-68). Herod had Him clothed, mockingly, in a robe (Luke 23:11). In Pilate's judgment hall "they clothed him with purple and platting a crown of thorns they put it on him, and they began to salute him, Hail, the king of the Jews! and they smote his head with a reed, and spat upon him, and bowing their knees worshipped him." (Mark 15:17-18). While He was on the cross, people railed on Him, wagging their heads and mocking Him (Mark 15:29-32).

14. Jesus predicted that it would be the Gentiles who put Him to death. This indicated that he would not die at the hands of the lawless mob like Stephen died. Although the chief priests would "condemn Him unto death," Jesus would be delivered unto the Gentiles who would put Him to death (Mark 10:33-34; Luke 18:31-32). When Jesus foretold His death by crucifixion this also implied that He would be delivered to the Gentiles, since crucifixion was a Roman, and not a Jewish, form of punishment and execution. It seemed unlikely, when Jesus made these predictions, that the Gentiles would put Him to death. The Roman rulers in Palestine and Jerusalem would not want to violate Roman justice by executing a Jew just because the religious leaders of Israel did not like him. The chief priests sometimes gave the Romans trouble, and this would make them all the less desirous of carrying out the wishes of the chief priests in this matter. Pilate did not want to put Jesus to death, for he realized Jesus was innocent (John 18:38). However, they finally prevailed upon Pilate and Pilate delivered Jesus, after he had scourged him, to be crucified (Luke 23:22-24).

15. Jesus foretold His resurrection (John 2:19-22; 10:17; Mark 10:34; Matt. 27:62-63; 1 Cor. 15:4). His resurrection is testified to by the Old Testament (Isaiah 53:10-12), by the Gospels, by Acts of Apostles and by the epistles of the New Testament. The existence of the church, baptism and the Lord's Supper all testify to it.

16. Jesus predicted His appearances, after His resurrection,

to the disciples. Jesus foresaw that the fury, which in the hearts of ungodly men had led to His death, would not also engulf and kill His disciples before His resurrection. They would live, and after His resurrection He knew He would appear to them. And this He did (Matt. 26:32; 28:16-17; Mark 16:14; John 21:1; 1 Corinthians. 15:5-6).

17. Jesus foretold his ascension into heaven (John 6:62; 16:28; 20:17). Luke and Paul testify to the reality of His ascension (Acts 1:9, 10; 9:9-16; 4:10).

18. Jesus predicted the coming of the Holy Spirit upon the apostles in Jerusalem (John 14:26; 16:7-14; Luke 24:49; Acts 1:8). Luke and the entire New Testament testify to its fulfillment (Acts 2:1-4).

19. Jesus promised the apostles they would be guided into all the truth (John 16:12-14). The context shows that reference was made to moral and spiritual truth. By the time the last apostle died, the entire New Testament had been written. It is the author's conviction that there is no moral and spiritual truth which cannot be found in express precept or broad principle in the Bible. If the reader thinks otherwise let him do the following. *First,* formulate a moral or religious truth which he thinks is new. *Second,* search the Scriptures to see if it is found therein. *Third,* if it is not found therein, let him give proof that it is a moral or religious truth. So far as the author's experiences have gone, he has seen no evidence which proves the reality of any new moral and religious truth. The author is confident that time and study will only underscore that Christ's teaching opposes, in precept or in principle, all evil and engenders, encourages, and nurtures all good.

20. Jesus predicted the establishment of His church or kingdom. Peter confessed the truth that Jesus is the Christ, and Jesus said: "Upon this rock I will build my church. " (Matt. 16:16, 18:19). It was to be a church, or kingdom, which was not of this world (John 18:36), whose members were to incorporate into their lives the principles of the sermon on the mount, and in which men should seek greatness through service rather than through being served (Matt. 20:20-28). How did He know that in spite of His death, and the scattering of His disciples, they would recover from their fright, and establish His church? Jesus promised it would be done in their lifetime (Mark 9:1). On the first Pentecost after Christ's resurrection, Jesus was proclaimed as ruling at God's right hand (Acts 2:36). His church (Eph. 1:19-23), His kingdom (Col. 1:13), continues to stand even unto this day.

21. Jesus predicted that His disciples would be persecuted by the Jews, put out of the synagogues, and some of them would be put to death (John 16:1-2). Luke gives us cases of such persecution (Acts 4:1; 7:1; 13:14, 50; 14:19).

22. Moses predicted the fall of Israel's walled cities, and this included the fall of her main city, Jerusalem. Jesus also prophesied that because of Israel's rebellion against God, Jerusalem would be destroyed. One of the places where the series of predictions, concerning Jerusalem's fall, is found in Matthew 24. Some of the predictions in Matthew 24 apply to the end of the world, some to the destruction of Jerusalem, and some could be applied to both since the judgment on Jerusalem typifies the final judgment of God on man.

> (a) The coming of false prophets who would deceive many before the city was destroyed (Matt. 24:4-5). Josephus tells us of some of them in his book on the *Jewish Wars,*
>
> (b) Persecution of Christ's disciples (Matt. 24:9-11). This happened both before and after the destruction of Jerusalem.
>
> (c) Jerusalem was to be so completely surrounded by armies that no one would be able to leave Jerusalem. "But when ye see Jerusalem compassed with armies, then

94

know that her desolation is at hand. " (Luke 21:20). "For the days shall come upon thee [Jerusalem, J.D.B.], when thine enemies shall cast up a bank (palisade, gr. margin) about thee, and compass thee round, and keep thee in on every side." (Luke 19:43). "A trench was literally cast about Jerusalem, when that city was besieged by Titus. The Roman armies compassed it round about completely; and although it was at first considered an impracticable project to surround the whole city with a wall, yet Titus animated his army to make the attempt. Josephus has given a very particular account of the building of this wall; which, he says, was effected in three days, though it was not less than thirty-nine furlongs (nearly nine English miles) in length, and had thirteen towers erected at proper distances, in which the Roman soldiers were placed, as in garrisons. When the wall was thus completed, the Jews were so enclosed on every side, that no person could escape out of the city, and no provision could be brought in: so that the besieged Jews were involved in the most terrible distress by the famine that ensued."[1]

(d)   The Jews would experience great tribulation (Luke 21:23-24). They perished by famine, disease, by their own hands and by the Roman sword. Even Caesar's soldiers grew tired of the slaughter.

(e)   The temple would be completely destroyed (Matt. 24:1-2). Titus wanted to spare it but he could not check his soldiers. It was destroyed and its foundations dug up.

(f)   The Jews were to be led captive after the fall (Luke

---

[1] T.H. Horne, *Introduction to the Scriptures, Vol.* I: 460. See this work for an examination of this prophecy in greater detail.

21:24). Multitudes were taken as slaves into all parts of the empire.

(g)   Jerusalem was to be trodden down until the times of the Gentiles were fulfilled (Luke 21:24).

(h)   When Jesus spoke His words, the temple seemed far more permanent than His words; words which may not seemed to have power reached to the walls of Jerusalem. He was a penniless and rejected teacher. He had no secretary to record His words. He also said that apostasies would take place even in the rank of His disciples. Yet, He prophesied that although the temple would pass, His word would not pass away (Matt. 24:33). His word has continued to stand, but the temple has ceased to exist.

(i)   Moses promised Israel that God would bless her if she turned from her iniquities and did the will of the Lord (Deut. 30). Jesus promised to bless those who did the will of the Lord (Matt. 23:37-39; 24:45-46).

AFTER THE TIME?

It may be objected that the prophecies of Jerusalem's destruction were made up after the fall of Jerusalem. To this we reply. *First,* as far as we know, no Jew or pagan in the early centuries reproached Christians with the assertion that these prophecies were invented after the events they described.

Second, the evidence which we have indicates that Matthew and Mark were written before the time of Jerusalem's destruction in AD 70. Although Stephen had not blasphemed Moses, the charges of certain Jews against him indicate that he likely had said something concerning the fall of Jerusalem (Acts 6:14). Acts would certainly have recorded Jerusalem's fall if it had fallen before Acts was written. Luke wrote his gospel before he wrote Acts (Acts 1:1).

Third, this charge assumes that the apostles and the rest of the members of the church were conscious liars. If Jesus had said anything about Jerusalem's fall, at least some of the disciples would have heard about it before AD 70. If a handful of disciples after AD 70 had said Jesus had prophesied the fall, but they had not told anyone about it, surely the other disciples would have been suspicious. Since some of the apostles, who had been close to Jesus, were living after the fall, they would have been able to expose such a fraud by pointing out that if Jesus had taught it, they would have heard these prophecies from His own lips instead of from someone else decades later. In other words, there is no reason to assume that most of the followers of Jesus were liars or that they would have been so easily imposed on by a few liars. When the Gospel accounts of the prediction of Jerusalem's fall were circulated there would be disciples living who had seen Jesus, as well as many who had been with those who had seen Jesus, and they would have known whether these prophecies had been heard of before the fall of Jerusalem. So even if all the Gospels had been written after Jerusalem's fall, it would still have been highly improbable that forged prophecies could have been palmed off on the church.

Fourth, although the author is convinced the Gospels do not contradict one another, if they had been forgeries they would certainly have removed at least some of the seeming inconsistencies. Furthermore, there are obscurities and difficulties in a very few of the prophecies in Matthew 24. If these were forgeries, it is likely they would not have been included. There would also have been a clearer line of demarcation between the statements, in certain instances, with reference to Jerusalem's fall and the ones which referred to the end of the world. As it is now, there are questions as to which events a few statements had in mind.

Fifth, certain of the predictions included things—such as the continuation of the downtrodden condition of Jerusalem—whose fulfillment did not take place in the first century.

PREDICTIONS FULFILLED OUTSIDE THE NEW TESTAMENT

(1) Jesus predicted that the Gentiles would hate and persecute His disciples for His name's sake (Matt. 10:22; 24:9-10; John 15:18-21). Richard Watson observed that: "Humanly speaking, the teachers of the Christian system had as fair a chance to be heard in the world, and to collect disciples among the civilized states around them, in an age of great and very free religious inquiry, as the followers of the various philosophic schools, and the founders of innumerable sects. Even Judaism had been widely propagated, and numbers of proselytes made from the Gentiles in various parts, without being followed by persecution on that account; and neither the Jews, who openly despised idolatry, nor the Epicurean sects, who denied a God and a providence, were molested. But our Lord knew the hearts of men everywhere, and how they would be affected by a religion, simple in its worship, humbling in its doctrines, terrible to sinners in its disclosures of a general judgment and future punishments, rigid in its moral discipline, and holding out to hope few, beside spiritual, blessings; he knew how the carnal mind, which is naturally enmity to God, would manifest itself when a religion of this character, and pressing upon it with the weight of this authority, should be everywhere introduced; and the event proved the infallibility of his knowledge, and the truth of his predictions."[2]

The time soon came when the disciples were persecuted by the Gentiles. "Tacitus affirms that the charge on which Christians were condemned (by Nero) was not incendiarism but 'hatred of mankind;' in other words, not for being criminals, but for being Chris-

---

[2] **Commentary on Matthew,** p. 342.

tians."[3] After Nero, the leading question which was still often asked of Christians was "Are thou a Christian?" "If the reply is in the affirmative, no further inquiry is needed; the crime is proved; condemnation will follow. That name alone carries within it the confession of gravest crimes, and is sufficient to bring down upon him who answers to it, odious suspicions of infamy, sacrilege, and rebellion.... To own to the name of Christian, was for the accused by implication to confess himself guilty of every crime. No investigation was necessary."[4]

When an individual would say: "I am a Christian," he knew that the mob would shout: "Death to the Christian!" For those who were faithful, "I am a Christian" was the only answer which they could give. As Maximus said to his judge: "I am a free man, *but* the slave of Christ."[5] When Ptolemaeus (in the second century) and Lucius answered that they were Christians they were led away to death.

Athenagoras, in 177 A.D., wrote thusly: "But why is a mere name odious to you? Names are not deserving of hatred: it is the unjust act that calls for penalty and punishment. And accordingly, with admiration for your mildness and gentleness and your peaceful and benevolent disposition towards every man, individuals live in the possession of equal rights; and the whole empire, under your intelligent sway, enjoys profound peace But for us who are called Christians you have not in like manner cared; but although we commit no wrong—nay, as will appear in the sequel of this discourse, are of all men most piously and righteously disposed towards the Deity and towards your government—you allow us to be harassed, plundered and persecuted, the multitude making war up-

---

[3] B.J. Kidd, **The History of the Church to A.D. 461**, Vol. I, pp. 57-58.

[4] E. de Pressense, **The Early Years of Christianity**, II, p. 87,

[5] *Ibid.*, p. 88.

on us for our name alone."

"It does not comport with your justice, that others when charged with crimes should not be punished till they are convicted, but that in our case the name we bear should have more force than the evidence adduced on the trial, when the judges, instead of inquiring whether the person arraigned have committed any crime, vent their insults on the name, as if that were itself a crime.... What therefore is conceded as the common right of all we claim for ourselves, that we shall not be hated and punished because we are called Christians (for what has the name to do with our being bad men?), but be tried on any charges which may be brought against us, and either be released on our disproving them, or punished if convicted of crime—not for the name (for no Christian is a bad man unless he falsely profess our doctrines), but for the wrong which has been done."[6]

Around 185 A.D. Apollonius stood before a Roman Prefect who said: "You have philosophized enough, and have filled us with admiration; but dost thou not know this, O Apollonius, that it is the decree of the Senate that no one shall be named a Christian anywhere at all? Apollonius answered, 'Aye, but it is not possible for a human decree of the Senate to prevail over the decree of God.'"[7]

Turtullian said: "Public hatred asks but one thing, and that, not investigation into the crimes charged, but simply the confession of the Christian name."[8] Thus we see that Christ foresaw that His disciples would not only be persecuted but that it would be for his "name's sake."

(2) Christ predicted the worldwide spread of the gospel. It was

---

[6] B. J. Kidd, **Documents Illustrative of the History of the Church,** London: S. P. C. K., 1920. I: 105-106.

[7] *Ibid*, p. 133.

[8] de Pressense, ***op. cit.,*** p. 88.

to be preached to all nations, beginning at Jerusalem (Matt. 28:18-20; Acts 1:8). B.W. Bond well said that "Nothing seemed then more unlikely to human foresight than this. Judea itself was but a small and despised country, and the Jews were everywhere held in detestation. How unlikely that a doctrine originating among Jews, and preached by Jews, without either the learning of the Greeks or the power of the Romans to recommend it, should yet find its way down the remotest ages of posterity, and throughout all nations! For Christ's doctrine was rejected even by the leaders of the Jewish nation itself, and He executed by them, and His followers persecuted, as also they afterwards were by the whole power of the Roman government, in ten great successive persecutions. How improbable did it seem that it could at all survive, when its own nation had disowned it, and was striving to stamp it out of existence; or, if it might linger obscurely among the hills and valleys of Galilee, how unlikely for it ever to spread abroad, even to the neighboring and kindred tribes; and how utterly impossible that it should ever prevail in distant continents, and among strange and unknown races of men! And what impostor would have dared to give by such a declaration such a test for succeeding ages, by which they might so easily expose and ridicule his claims? Yet, standing where we are today, we behold the preaching of the gospel fast extending to every land under heaven."[9]

(3) Christ predicted that His church would be international in character. When one studies the prejudices of the Jews against foreigners one wonders how Christ could have so overcome that prejudice that His disciples, who were at first drawn from the rank of the Jews, would carry the gospel to the Gentiles. The Jews had no dealings with the Samaritans (John 4:9). Alfred Edersheim has pointed out the animosity which existed between the Jews and the

---

[9] B.*W.* Bond, **The Positive Evidence of Christianity**, pp. 203-204.

Samaritans. "On all public occasions the Samaritans took the part hostile to the Jews, while they seized every opportunity of injuring and insulting them." "The Jews retaliated by treating the Samaritans with every mark of contempt; by accusing them of falsehood, folly, and irreligion; and what they felt most keenly, by disowning them as of the same race or religion, and this in the most offensive terms of assumed superiority and self-righteous fanaticism."[10] With reference to the Gentiles the Jews did not even consider it lawful to eat with them. Their abhorrence of all that was connected with idolatry, and the contempt entertained for all that was non-Jewish, will in great measure explain the code of legislation intended to keep the Jew and Gentile apart."[11] Edersheim illustrates the various ways in which this separation was indicated. Even after the establishment of the church there were multitudes of Christians for many years who did not think that it was lawful to eat with the Gentiles (Acts 11). So deep-seated was their prejudice, carried over from their former life under Judaism, that it took special miracles to convince the church that the gospel was for the Gentile on the same basis as for the Jews. And yet, it was to people with such prejudices that Jesus committed the gospel and said that it was to be taken to all nations (Mark 16:15-16; Matt. 28:18-20). Christ knew their prejudice and yet into their hands He committed His work. He Himself, in person, did not go to the Gentiles. But, His disciples finally went. In fact, after the Spirit revealed the truth of the spiritual nature of the church to them, they taught that "there is neither Jew nor Greek, there is neither bond nor free, there is neither male nor female; for ye are all one in Christ Jesus." (Gal. 3:28). It certainly took a prophet to see that the church would be international and it took the guidance of the Spirit and miracles in

---

[10] Alfred Edersheim, **The Life and Times of Jesus the** Messiah, I: 399
[11] *Ibid.*, **p.** 90.

order to convince the church that such was its character. We today know how hard it is to overcome racial prejudices.

(4) Jesus said that His Kingdom would endure until the end of the world (Matt. 13:24-50; 28:20). Babylon was in the dust when Jesus spoke these words. He knew kingdoms had risen, waxed, and waned. He knew that He was a person unknown to the world as a whole. The mighty Caesars reigned on their thrones in Jesus' day. Yet they have long ago passed on, and their kingdoms came to an end. Jesus' kingdom still stands, and in spite of all the enemies arrayed against it today, and in spite of the persecution which it has received and which it will receive, it will continue to stand.

(5) Jesus predicted the power and influence of His death. What the world would view as the end of His career, and as a career that ended with defeat, Jesus said would be a powerful source of His influence and victory (John 12:23-24, 32).

William H. Thomson well said: "For what is the underlying, sustaining principle of the Church—that which has maintained her existence and growth throughout the varying times? Unquestionably it is the dogma of the death and resurrection of Jesus. It is this alone which keeps Christianity alive. If the central significance of this doctrine be removed, there remains to Christianity but a mutilated system of ethics, no more capable of affecting the world, or of holding multitudes of every race to a life-and-death devotion, than ethics is capable of leading men to any self-sacrifice, say, in honor of Socrates or Seneca. Without the Cross and the Resurrection, men would have no more reason to serve Jesus than to serve Socrates. On the other hand, the apprehension of the meaning and results of that Death and Resurrection must profoundly modify men. After being convinced that the Cross bore the Son of God, no one can regard the problems of life in the same light as before.

"The doctrine of the Cross has always been revolutionary with persons, and hence, sooner or later, with society. The 'offence of the Cross' is, therefore, no figurative expression, for everyone feels instinctively that to believe in it involves an adjustment of the whole life accordingly. There can be no neutral course between a wholehearted acceptance, or an equally determined rejection of its claims, and for this reason it has stirred men and nations as no system of philosophy or ethics has ever been able to do. For influence exerted, even unbelievers must admit that its entrance into the world is the most momentous fact of the ages.

"Regarded, however, from a natural standpoint, this doctrine is so strange and unique that it is impossible that anyone could have invented it, or foreseen its incalculable results. Like Jesus Himself, it stands alone. The work of men must cease at death, and only the influences from their previous lives can continue. But here it is Christ's death which we find transforming the terrified fishermen into the apostles, who had power to move the world. That which was naturally regarded by His enemies as the end, was in fact an infinitely greater beginning than anyone then in the world could have understood.

"But all this was distinctly foreseen and foretold by Jesus. He never mistook the future. In repeated instances His words proved that He looked to overturning all things, not by His life, but by His death. He came, according to His own account, to set mankind at variance, to send, not peace, but a sword, to cast fire on the earth, but He was to accomplish this by being put to death (Matt. 10:34-39; Luke 12:49). He certainly, therefore, did not underrate His own personality. The cross was not to make Him; He was to make the cross. His language is that of one who knows that He will shake the world—not that of His day only, but the world of all future history—to its foundations, and this by means of the Roman gibbet for criminals. 'The hour is come, that the Son of man should be glorified. Verily, verily, I say unto you, Except a grain of wheat fall into the earth and die, it abideth by itself alone; but if it die, it beareth much fruit... And I, if I be lifted up from the earth, will draw all men unto myself.' (John 12:23-24, 32). This, we are told, He said signifying what death He should die.

"It is His death and resurrection, therefore, which constitutes His sole answer to the challenge for evidence [Christ pointed to other credentials also. John 5:33-47; 20:30-31, etc. J.D.B.]. In support of His unprecedented claims, it was demanded of Him to adduce a sign which should make men dumb. He does so, leaving history to seal His words. No sign but this: 'The Son of man shall be three days and three nights in the heart of the earth' (Matt. 12. 40). When again asked for proof, His answer was, 'Destroy this temple, and in three days I will raise it up' (John 2:19). That His words had a meaning His adversaries well knew; but the future alone could explain it.

"That future has explained it. How can the opposer answer this sign now? From age to age the belief in the death and resurrection of Jesus has caused, in various ways, such general and personal conflict, that it is impossible to do more than allude to it. If opposition could destroy, it has always been opposed. The Jewish rulers thoroughly disbelieved and scorned the idea that He who hung upon the Cross was other than a Galilean peasant, but not more thoroughly than men like Julian, and Paine, and Strauss, and multitudes in every age have likewise done. Nothing in the past or present is so disbelieved in as the Cross. It is a sign always spoken against (Luke 2:34-35). But how is it to be explained? Until the believer can show why it is that the death of Jesus has made him live, against constant opposition, as the most constant power of history, he need not ask us for another sign.

"This proof that Jesus was a prophet cannot be evaded by the objector on the supposition that He Himself did not foresee the place to be held in the world by the Cross, and that His prophetic utterances are the inventions of His disciples, made for the purpose of neutralizing His sudden and impotent end. They invent the extraordinary paradox of a victorious execution! But how came they to believe in such a victory, even to the extent of being crucified themselves in testimony to it? If Jesus were not a prophet in speaking as He did of the historical importance of His death, it follows that His disciples were so. They chose it for a sign to the world, and committed themselves to the statement that this—in their day—very ordinary event, the crucifixion of a Galilean, was to draw all men to him! Is it not easier to admit that it must have been their unexampled Master who foretold this unexampled wonder of all time?

"There is something profoundly impressive in the tone of language constantly employed by Jesus in regard to the future. It is to be observed not only in especial utterances, though these also there are, but in the calm assumption of his own deathless presence in the world. He is to die, and yet to live, with the coming ages always before him, in a literal, not a figurative, sense. At the close of that terrible denunciation of the men who were leading the doomed nation to ruin, recorded in the twenty- third chapter of Matthew, he spake as never man spoke, thus: 'Therefore, behold, I send unto you prophets, and wise men, and scribes, some of them shall ye kill and crucify; and some of them shall ye scourge in your synagogues, and persecute from city to city.... O Jerusalem, Jerusalem, that killeth the prophets, and stoneth them that are sent unto her! how often would I have gathered thy children together, even as a hen gathereth her chickens under her wings, and ye would not! Behold, your house is left unto you desolate. For I say unto you, Ye shall not see me henceforth, till ye shall say. Blessed is he that cometh in the name of the Lord.' (Matt. 23:34, 37). We know with certainty that he who spoke thus like God, of sending prophets and wise men and scribes for that generation to slay, meant also to predict that Jerusalem was to be destroyed, and the Jewish people

106

scattered for centuries before they should see him again, because his answer to his anxious disciples as to what it was which he then foretold, is contained in the following chapter.

"The discourse in Luke which belongs to this juncture likewise contains the remarkable instructions for the future which Jesus gave to his apostles in the tenth chapter of Matthew. On at least three successive occasions during his ministry did Jesus put his disciples to the training which was to fit them for going into the world and preaching, when he should be no longer with them, telling them, at the same time of the fate which awaited them. 'Behold, I send you forth as sheep in the midst of wolves: be ye therefore wise as serpents and harmless as doves. But beware of men: for they will deliver you up to councils, and in their synagogues they will scourge you; yea and before governors and kings shall ye be brought for my sake.' (Matt. 10:16-18). The hearing and the dealing which should be accorded by the world to his messengers lay all before Him who, we are told by some was only a carpenter of Nazareth. His fishermen were to stand before kings, because it would be a matter of importance to kings that they should be brought before them. 'I will make you fishers of men,' He had aforetime said to those same poor ignorant Galileans, and now kings' courts and the capitals of empires are named in their honor.

"In that future, also, He saw His claims causing every other claim, even the closest of earth, to be as nothing, among men of every race, though life itself were the price of this allegiance. But such devotion and such opposition have followed His name from age to age. The prophecies of the hidden treasure and the pearl of great price have been fulfilled in the case of thousands through centuries, and the world has witnessed the growth of the mustard-seed, and felt the working of the leaven. It has seen as well the ceaseless marvel of the devout acceptance by its leading races, from Jewish hands, of that kingdom fatally rejected by the Jewish people, fulfilled thereby another of the prophetic parables of Jesus, that of the Vineyard. 'Therefore say I unto you, the kingdom of God shall be taken away from you, and shall be given to a nation bringing forth the fruits thereof. And he that falleth on this stone shall be broken to pieces: but on whomsoever it shall fall, it will scatter him as dust,' (Matt. 21:43-44).

"What utterance of Jesus can be quoted as proof that He did not know the future? Although the writings of every wise man of every nation show conclusively of how little worth is human wisdom in attempting prophecy, nevertheless, who can convince Jesus of error while He looks constantly beyond the horizon possible to a Galilean peasant over all the expanse of time? Does not this ever present sign in Jesus prove that He is, in truth, the Prophet sent by Him who also warns men that He will require it of them who hearken not to a messenger whom He has so accredited?"[12]

(6) Jesus prophesied the moral and spiritual influence of His own person. "I am the light of the world; he that followeth me shall not walk in the darkness, but shall have the light of life." (John 8:12). These words, uttered while He was an obscure teacher of a despised race, are the words of an unbalanced fanatic, to say the least, or of the Son of God, which He claimed to be. His claim can be evaluated in the light of history as well as of personal experience. C.A. Row has delineated this argument at length in the *Bampton Lectures,* 1877, and in his *Manual of Christian Evidence.* Spiritual and moral life is generated by Him and His word. "He is the moral and spiritual illuminator at this present moment of all the progressive nations on earth; and all who are not walking in His light are fallen into a state of stagnation and decay" or of brutal

---

[12] William H. Thomson, *The Great Argument or Jesus Christ in the Old Testament,* New York: Harper and Brothers, Franklin Square 1884 pp. 161-166.

moral degradation. Where men have allowed the light of His life and word to shine, political, social and moral life have been elevated and ennobled.

If we had space we could present the testimony of eminent men, both unbelievers and believers, to the moral and spiritual superiority of Jesus. We could also present the testimony of followers of other religions as well as the testimony of individual lives which have been raised from a debased condition to a holy one. Lecky, Rousseau, John Stuart Mill, Renan, Matthew Arnold, Goethe, Jean Paul Richter, Spinoza, Kant, Jacobi, Schelling, Hegel, Thomas Carlyle, Herder, and a multitude of others seemed to have vied with one another in their efforts to frame a fitting tribute to Christ. The world still has not touched the hem of His garment insofar as approaching His teachings is concerned. *The marvel is not only that this has happened but that He predicted that it would happen.* He makes the most tremendous affirmation that could come from the lips of man and two thousand years of history testifies to His light and life-giving power and back up His affirmations.

(7) He said that men must build on His word or their structure would not stand (Matt. 7:24-27). The sorry sights which we view in today's world testify to the fact that the world must walk the way which He Himself pointed out and walked or that it will walk to its own self-destruction.

These examples of the prophetic power of Jesus indicate that He was more than a mere human speculator. They confirm the tone of authority with which He spoke. But we do not have to appeal to the testimony of the past alone. Individuals who are willing to try Him, to stake their all upon His way of life, will discover that He spoke the truth when He said that, though it would get one into trouble with the unregenerate, it would lead to the fulfillment of that which is highest in man as well as to inward peace. Try Him.

He won't let you down. But give Him an honest, fair and sincere trial.

To get a full view of the predictions of Jesus, we would have to consider the prophecies uttered by the apostles and prophets of the New Testament; for they were guided by the Spirit whom Jesus sent. Their predictions may be said to be His predictions also. However, we have referred to sufficient predictions to indicate that in this respect also Jesus is the prophet like unto Moses.

CHAPTER 7

Required of Them

Moses did not prophesy that everyone would hearken unto the prophet like unto himself. Instead, he indicated some would not obey and that they would be held accountable. "And it shall come to pass, that whosoever will not hearken unto my words which he shall speak in my name, I will require it of him" (Deut. 18:19). Joseph Reider, Professor of Biblical Philology, Dropsie College, interpreted the verse by saying: "I will exact punishment of the man who disobeys the prophet's message. The penalty, according to the Jewish tradition, is death by the hand of God (Sifre)."[1] This interpretation is also found in the Talmud.[2] The book of Acts shows that the disobedient were to be cut off from God's people. "And it shall be, that every soul that shall not hearken to that prophet, shall be utterly destroyed from among the people" (Acts 3:23).

Has it been, and will it be, required of those who refuse to listen to Jesus the Messiah?

JESUS WARNED ISRAEL

Since Christ is the prophet like unto Moses, to reject Him is to invite the wrath of God. Therefore, Christ warned Israel of the consequences of rejecting Him.

"Hear another parable: There was a man that was a house-

---

[1] Joseph Reider, **Deuteronomy with Commentary,** Philadelphia: The Jewish Publication Society of America, 1948, p. 181.

[2] Isidore Epstein, Editor, **The Babylonian Talmud,** London: Soncino Press, 1935-48. Translated into English with notes, glossary, and indices. **Sanhedrin,** Part 4, v. 6, p. 89a,

holder, who planted a vineyard, and set a hedge about it, and digged a wine-press in it, and built a tower, and let it out to husbandmen, and went into another country. And when the season of the fruits drew near, he sent his servants to the husbandmen, to receive his fruits. And the husbandmen took his servants and beat one, and killed another, and stoned another. Again, he sent other servants more than the first: and they did unto them in like manner. But afterward he sent unto them his son, saying, They will reverence my son. But the husbandmen, when they saw the son, said among themselves, This is the heir; come, let us kill him and take his inheritance. And they took him, and cast him forth out of the vineyard, and killed him. When therefore the lord of the vineyard shall come, what will he do unto those husbandmen? They say unto him, He will miserably destroy those miserable men, and will let out the vineyard unto other husbandmen, who shall render him the fruits in their seasons. Jesus saith unto them, Did ye never read in the scriptures, The stone which the builders rejected the same was made the head of the corner; This was from the Lord and it is marvelous in our eyes? Therefore say I unto you, The kingdom of God shall be taken away from you, and shall be given to a nation bringing forth the fruits thereof. And he that falleth on this stone shall be broken to pieces: but on whomsoever it shall fall, it will scatter him as dust. And when the chief priests and the Pharisees heard his parables, they perceived that he spake of them. And when they sought to lay hold on him, they feared the multitudes, because they took him for a prophet." (Matt 21:33-46).

Have they been cut off? Has it been required of them? The New Testament church is a spiritual kingdom. Unlike the Old Testament system, God's people today do not constitute a theocracy which combines church and state. As a spiritual kingdom, God's church, God's nation, today does not have the power of life or death. Therefore they do not mete out physical punishment to those who reject the gospel or to those who are unfaithful in the church. However, although the church does not require it of those who reject Christ, God has required it of Israel and ultimately will require it of all the disobedient. How?

CUT OFF FROM COVENANT RELATIONSHIP

A remnant of the nation of Israel accepted Christ, but the majority rejected Him and were rejected of God (Rom. 10:1-5; 11:1-5). Paul taught that Israel had been cut off from covenant relationship with God because of her rejection of the Lord Jesus Christ. Warning the Gentiles, who had come into covenant relationship, against boasting, he said:

> *"Thou wilt say then, Branches were broken off, that I might be grafted in. Well; by their unbelief they were broken off, and thou standest by thy faith. Be not high-minded, but fear: for if God spared not the natural branches, neither will he spare thee. Behold the goodness and severity of God: toward them that fell, severity; but toward thee, God's goodness, if thou continue in his goodness: otherwise thou also shalt be cut off. And they also, if they continue not in their unbelief, shall be grafted in: for God is able to graft them in again." (Rom. 11:19-23).*

Israel did not hearken unto the words of the prophet like unto Moses, and, therefore, they were cut off from covenant relationship with God.

The reader may object that the Jews do not believe that they have been cut off from covenant relationship with God. They reject Paul, and his statements do not prove to them that they are actually cut off; therefore, it is not proved that their rejection of Jesus was required of them by God. What shall we say to this? *First*, during the personal ministry of Christ, and for a while after the establishment of the church, Israel had a temple and continued her worship, as authorized by the old covenant, in Jerusalem. But since that time they have been, as a whole, cast out of the land, and the temple worship has of necessity been abandoned. *Second*, since the worship prescribed in the old covenant was necessary, the failure to adhere to it means that they have broken the covenant and are out of covenant relationship with God. They are not keeping the worship today which was prescribed in the Old Testament. They could not even if they all wanted to do so. By making it impossible, for around two thousands of years, for them to worship as prescribed in the old covenant, God has made it clear that the old covenant has been abolished.

Multitudes of people are hearkening unto Christ, but no one today hearkens unto Moses and his law; and neither can they do so. The prophet like unto Moses has come and Moses has been replaced. Those who do not accept the Messiah cannot enter into covenant relationship with God. They cannot go back to Moses, and if they do not go to the Messiah there is no one to whom they can go as a mediator between man and God. To reject the new covenant is to be without a covenant, for God has no other covenant today.

SUBJECTED TO WRATH

Although Israel rejected Jesus Christ, God did not require it of them immediately but for around forty years He stayed His hand of wrath; and Israel had the gospel preached to her. But Israel not only rejected Jesus while He was on earth, but she also rejected the message taught by the apostles and prophets whom Christ sent. Jesus said:

> *"Therefore, behold, I send unto you prophets, and wise men, and scribes: some of them shall ye kill and crucify: and some of them shall ye scourge in your synagogues, and persecute from city to city: that upon you may come all the righteous blood shed on the earth, from the blood of Abel the righteous unto the blood of Zachariah son of Barachiah, whom ye slew between the sanctuary and the altar. Verily I say unto you, All these things shall come upon this generation.*

> *"O Jerusalem, Jerusalem, that killeth the prophets, and stoneth them that are sent unto her! how often would I have gathered thy children together, even as a hen gathereth her chickens under her wings, and ye would not! Behold, your house is left unto you desolate. For I say unto you, Ye shall not see me henceforth, till ye shall say, Blessed is he that cometh in the name of the Lord." (Matt. 23:34-39).*

Moses prophesied that if Israel disobeyed the prophet, God would require if of them (Deut. 18:19). He presented in great detail some of the judgments of God which would come upon them if they took the path of disobedience. They would be attacked by a nation whom they had not known in Moses' time, they would be plucked up off the land, scattered throughout the nations of the earth, be greatly reduced in number, they would not be utterly destroyed, they would not find lasting peace and rest, they would become a hiss and a by-word, a proverb, a sign, and an astonishment (Deut. 28). Jesus also foretold some of the consequences of their disobedience, such as the destruction of Jerusalem (Matt. 24).

Regardless of how one may try to explain these predictions, it is a matter of fact—not opinion—that the Jews have suffered those things which both Moses and the Messiah predicted. Although the Old Testament records some instances when Israel fell into idolatry, and came under the judgment of God, none of the judgments in the Old Testament times have equaled the judgments which have come on Israel since their rejection of Jesus. These judgments have not come because Israel became an idolatrous nation, for neither in Jesus' day nor thereafter has she gone into idolatry as she did in certain instances in Old Testament times. Although no Jew has been able to keep the Law of Moses since the destruction of the temple, the Jews have endeavored to keep at least certain aspects of the law. In many cases they have been persecuted because they refused to give up these observances and merge with the people around them. Many of the insults and persecutions "appear to be the *consequence* of their keeping to their religion, and not of their forsaking it.... So that the Jews of the present day seem to be suffering, for their *observance* of the law, just the penalties threatened for their departure from it."

How can this be? The Old Testament teaches that if they did not hearken unto the prophet like unto Moses, God would require it of them (Deut. 18:15-19; Acts 3:22-23). "Now *we* hold that the Jews have been guilty of this very act of disobedience in rejecting the Christ. And though they, of course, do not confess themselves thus guilty, because they deny that Jesus of Nazareth was the true Christ, yet they so far agree with us as to acknowledge, that the rejecting of the true Christ on his coming would be such a sin as would expose them to the judgments which Moses threatened."

Since their rejection of Jesus Christ, the entire series of calamities prophesied by Moses have come upon them. Moses said that these would not happen unless they disobeyed God, and he promised them numerous blessings if they walked in the path of obedience. These things have happened to them; therefore, they must have taken the path of disobedience. They rejected Jesus, and it has been required of them; as Moses foretold. Although many of them may want to keep the old covenant, with its temple system, it has been impossible for them to do so; and this impossibility started shortly after they rejected Jesus.

"Let a Jew explain, if he can, how it is that for so long a time Providence has put it out of the power of the Jews to observe the principal part of their religion, which they maintain was intended to be observed forever."

The very nature of the old covenant, with its temple in Jerusalem, meant that the old covenant could be abolished against the will of Israel. Christianity, if forbidden by law, can continue its system of worship underground; or Christians can flee from one country to another, Judaism, in its nature, was not such a religion. It was tied in with a particular land and temple. "It seems to have been designed and contrived by Divine Providence, that, as their *law* was to be brought to an end by the Gospel (for which it was a preparation), so all men were to *perceive* that it did come to an end, notwithstanding the obstinate rejection of the Gospel by the great part of the Jews. It was not left to be a question, and a matter of *opinion,* whether the sacrifices instituted by Moses were to be continued or not; but things were so ordered as to put it out of man's power to continue them."[3]

WILL ISRAEL ASK WHY?

In all of God's judgments on Israel in Old Testament times, she was never so long under judgment as she has been since the rejection of Jesus. What disobedience, persisted in, has so overshadowed the disobediences in Old Testament times that God's disfavor has been so long on Israel? Her long abandonment by God

---

[3] Whately, *Lessons on* Morals *and Christian Evidences,* Cambridge: John Bartlett, 1856, pp. 292, 293, 295, 296.

and her inability to keep the covenant is sufficient proof that she is not in covenant relationship with God and not under God's favor—should lead her to examine anew her past to see whether or not it is being required of them because they did not hearken unto the prophet like unto Moses.

That some have raised this question is indicated by an unnamed Jewish writer who said:

"There is nothing steady in Jewish life because the Jew has not found an anchor ground. We have been blind to the lessons of our history. Remember what happened to our forefathers when they lusted exceedingly in the wilderness and tempted God in the desert. He gave them their request; but sent leanness into their soul. Have the rabbis given us the answer to our everlastingly repeated question, 'Why have we suffered?'... Are we not still in the dark concerning our Messiah? Can we be delivered without Him? The answers to our many perplexing questions have not been forthcoming from the pulpits of the 3,000 synagogues of America."

"All the curses that the prophets foretold would be our lot have come to pass in a most remarkably accurate manner. Back to the prophets!"[4]

HEARKEN

When one goes back to the prophets, the prophets send one to Christ who is the prophet like unto Moses, and to whom the people should hearken. Men were held accountable under the law. How much more are they held accountable to hearken unto the prophet like unto Moses! This is the theme of the book of Hebrews. God speaks to us today through His Son, in contrast with the message which went to the fathers through the prophets (Heb. 1:1-2).

---

[4] As quoted by Ernest Gordon, "A Survey of Religious Life and Thought," *The Sunday School Times,* May 23, 1950, p. 408.

"Therefore we ought to give the more earnest heed to the things that were heard, lest haply we drift away from them. For if the word spoken through angels proved steadfast, and every transgression and disobedience received a just recompense of reward; how shall we escape, if we neglect so great a salvation? which having at the first been spoken through the Lord, was confirmed unto us by them that heard; God also bearing witness with them, both by signs and wonders, and by manifold powers, and by gifts of the Holy Spirit, according to his own will." (Heb. 2:1-4).

"Wherefore, holy brethren, partakers of a heavenly calling, consider the Apostle and High Priest of our confession, even Jesus; who was faithful to him that appointed him, as also was Moses in all his house. For he hath been counted worthy of more glory than Moses, by so much as he that built the house hath more honor than the house. For every house is builded by someone, but he that built all things is God, And Moses indeed was faithful in all his house as a servant, for a testimony of those things which were afterward to be spoken; but Christ as a son, over his house; whose house are we, if we hold fast our boldness and the glorying of our hope firm unto the end." (Heb. 3:1-6).

"We have an altar, whereof they have no right to eat that serve the tabernacle. For the bodies of those beasts whose blood is brought into the holy place by the high priest as an offering for sin, are burned without the camp. Wherefore Jesus also, that he might sanctify the people through his own blood, suffered without the gate. Let us therefore go forth unto him without the camp, bearing his reproach. For we have not here an abiding city, but we seek after the city which is to come. Through him then let us offer up a sacri-

fice of praise to God continually, that is, the fruit of lips which make confession to his name. But to do good and to communicate forget not: for with such sacrifices God is well pleased." (Heb. 13:10-16).

One must turn from Moses unto the Messiah in order to be in covenant relationship with God today. To reject the Messiah and His covenant is to reject Moses, for he prophesied of Christ, and is to place one under the judgment of God. It will be required of him.

CHAPTER 8

The Prophet Like Unto Moses

What Moses promised, Christ fulfilled.

> *"Jehovah thy God will raise up unto thee a prophet from the midst of thee, of thy brethren, like unto me; unto him ye shall hearken; according to all that thou desired of Jehovah thy God in Horeb in the day of the assembly, saying, Let me not hear again the voice of Jehovah my God, neither let me see this great fire any more, that I die not. And Jehovah said unto me, They have well said that which they have spoken. I will raise them up a prophet from among their brethren, like unto thee; and I will put my words in his mouth, and he shall speak unto them all that I shall command him. And it shall come to pass, that whosoever will not hearken unto my words which he shall speak in my name, I will require it of him."* (Deut. 18:15-19).

JESUS AN ISRAELITE

The prophet like unto Moses was not to be a foreigner but was to be an Israelite. Although Jesus is divine as well as human, according to the flesh He was the offspring of David (Isa. 9:6-7; Matt. 1:1-17; Acts 2:30; Rom. 1:3). Jesus came before the genealogical records of Israel were totally destroyed, and, therefore, He came while it was still possible to trace with certainty whether one was of Israel.

LIKE UNTO MOSES

Of all the prophets of Israel since Moses the only one truly like unto Moses is Jesus of Nazareth. How is He like Moses? *First,* the law was given by Moses, but it was only a shadow of that which was to be given through Christ (John 1:17; Col. 2:14-17; Heb. 10:1). Christ has given us the law of the Spirit of life which makes us free (Rom. 8:2; 1 Cor. 9:21; Heb. 8:10).

Second, Moses was the mediator of the old covenant and Christ is the mediator of the new covenant (Jer. 31:31-34; Heb. 8:5-13; 12:24; 13:20).

Third, Moses was the great deliverer of the Jews; the physical Israel who made up God's people in Moses' day. Christ is the great spiritual deliverer of God's spiritual Israel; those who are delivered by Him from bondage to sin.

Fourth, in order to confirm Moses' authority and to make possible Israel's deliverance, Moses wrought mighty miracles. None of the other prophets in the Old Testament were like him "in all the signs and the wonders, which Jehovah sent him to do in the land of Egypt, to Pharaoh, and to all his servants, and to all his land, and in all the mighty hand, and in all the great terror, which Moses wrought in the sight of all Israel." (Deut. 34:11-12). Christ's ministry, and the ministry of the apostles and prophets whom He sent and whose work was a continuation and confirmation of His word, was accompanied by a larger number and greater variety of miraculous works. His miracles not only confirmed His word, but the miracles (such as the resurrection, ascension, and sending of the Spirit) were also involved in making possible our spiritual deliverance from bondage to sin.

Fifth, both Moses and Christ foretold many things which were to come.

THE CONTEXT OF HIS MESSAGE

At least part of the message of Moses was delivered in such a fear-producing context that the people asked that they not hear again, directly, the voice of Jehovah; nor hear and see the fearful demonstrations. This request was granted, and the people were told, furthermore, that the prophet like unto Moses would not place His message in the context of such fearful demonstrations (Deut. 5:22-28; 18:16-17). The Sermon on the Mount, for example, was not in the context of thunder, lightning, the smoking mountain, and the audible voice of God.

GOD'S WORD IN THE PROPHET'S MOUTH

God promised to put His words in the prophet's mouth, and the prophet would be faithful in speaking unto the people all that God commanded the prophet. Jesus emphasized that the word which He spoke was the word which He received from the Father (John 8:28; 12:48-50; 16:12-15; 17:8). Christ's words are worthy of God. If God has spoken anywhere, we can rest assured that He has spoken in and through Christ. If Christ's word is not God's word, it is futile to look elsewhere for a word from God. We cannot answer all questions and solve all problems, and at times we may be perplexed over some matters. However, we are not like those who turned back because of some difficulties. After Jesus had uttered some sayings which were hard, "upon this many of his disciples went back, and walked no more with him. Jesus said therefore unto the twelve, Would ye also go away? Simon Peter answered him, Lord, to whom shall we go? thou hast the words of eternal life. And we have believed and know that thou art the Holy One of God." (John 6:66-69).

REQUIRED OF THEM

God speaks to us through the prophet like unto Moses; therefore, to reject this prophet is to reject God's word. God said that He would hold men accountable and that "it shall come to pass, that whosoever will not hearken unto my word which he shall speak in my name, I will require it of him." (Deut. 18:19). Those of Israel, who rejected His word, had it required of them. They were cut off from covenant relationship with God, and Jerusalem and the temple were destroyed. Whether they would have it so or not, the old covenant has not been in force for around two thousand years. They have not kept it, and they cannot keep it now. Those who reject Him today cannot enter into covenant relationship with God, and, they, with rejectors of all generations, shall someday have it required of them when they face Christ in judgment. Men shall be judged by Him and His word (John 12:48; Acts 17:30-31).

The prophet like unto Moses has come! Will you hearken unto Him? (Acts 2:30-42).

A Host of Likenesses

We have presented in this book those likenesses which we believe are basic in showing that Jesus is the prophet like unto Moses. However, there are many other points of similarity which, although not essential in proving that Jesus is that prophet, are yet not without interest. The following section has been taken verbatim from a book by Thomas Newton.

NEWTON ON THE LIKENESSES

"We shall be more and more confirmed in this opinion, when we consider the great and striking likeness between Moses and Jesus Christ, and that the latter resembled the former in more respects than any other person ever did. Notice has been taken already of some instances, wherein they resemble each other, of God speaking to both, 'face to face,' of both performing 'signs and wonders,' of both being 'lawgivers:' and in these respects none of the ancient prophets were like unto Moses. None of them were lawgivers; they only interpreted and enforced the Law of Moses. None of them performed so many and so great wonders. None of them had such clear communications with God; they all saw visions, and dreamed dreams. Moses and Jesus Christ are the only two who perfectly resemble each other in these respects. But a more exact and particular comparison may be drawn between them, and has been drawn by two eminent hands, by one of the best and ablest of the ancient fathers, and by one of the most learned and ingenious of modern divines: and as we cannot pretend to add anything to them, we must be content to copy from them.

"Eusebius treating of the prophecies concerning Christ, produces first this of Moses: and then asks, which of the prophets after Moses, Isaiah for instance, or Jeremiah, or Ezekiel, or Daniel, or any other of the twelve, was a lawgiver, and performed things like unto Moses? Moses first rescued the Jewish nation from Egyptian superstition and idolatry, and taught them the true theology; Jesus Christ in like manner was the first teacher of true religion and virtue to the Gentiles. Moses confirmed his religion by miracles: and so likewise did Christ. Moses delivered the Jewish nation from Egyptian servitude; and Jesus Christ all mankind from the power of evil demons. Moses promised a holy land, and therein a happy life to those who kept the law; and Jesus Christ a better country, that is, a heavenly, to all righteous souls. Moses fasted forty days; and so likewise did Christ. Moses supplied the people with bread in the wilderness: and our Savior fed five thousand at one time, and four thousand at another with a few loaves. Moses went himself, and led the people through the midst of the sea; and Jesus Christ walked on the sea, and enabled Peter to walk likewise. Moses stretched out his hand over the sea, and the Lord caused the sea to go backward; and our Savior rebuked the wind and the sea, and there was a great calm. Moses's face shone, when he descended from the mount; and our Savior's did shine as the sun in his transfiguration. Moses by his prayers cured Miriam of her leprosy; and Christ with greater power by a word healed several lepers. Moses performed wonders by the finger of God; and Jesus Christ by the finger of God did cast out devils. Moses changed Oshea's name to Joshua; and our Savior did Simon's to Peter. Moses constituted seventy rulers over the people; and our Savior appointed seventy disciples. Moses sent forth twelve men to spy out the land; and our Savior twelve apostles to visit all nations. Moses gave several excellent moral precepts; and our Savior carried them to the highest perfection.

"Dr. Jortin has enlarged upon these hints of Eusebius and made several improvements and additions to them. Moses in his infancy was wonderfully preserved from the destruction of all the male children; so was Christ. Moses fled from his country to escape the hands of the king; so did Christ, when his parents carried him into Egypt: afterwards 'the Lord said to Moses in Midian, Go, return into Egypt; for all the men are dead which sought thy life,' Exod. 4:19; so the angel of the Lord said to Joseph, in almost the same words, 'Arise, and take the young child, and go into the land of Israel; for they are dead which sought the young child's life,'— Matt. 2:20; pointing him out as it were for that prophet, who should arise like unto Moses. Moses refused to be called the son of Pharaoh's daughter, choosing rather to suffer affliction; Christ refused to be made king, choosing rather to suffer affliction. Moses, says St. Stephen, 'was learned in all the wisdom of the Egyptians,' and Josephus, *Ant. Jud.* 2.9, says, that he was a very forward and accomplished youth, and had wisdom and knowledge beyond his years; St. Luke observes of Christ, that 'he increased (betimes) in wisdom and stature, and in favor with God and man,' and his discourses in the temple with the doctors, when he was twelve years old, were a proof of it. Moses contended with the magicians, who were forced to acknowledge the divine power by which he was assisted; Christ rejected evil spirits, and received the same acknowledgements from them. Moses was not only a lawgiver, a prophet, and a worker of miracles, but a king and a priest; in all these offices the resemblance between Moses and Christ was singular. Moses brought darkness over the land; the sun withdrew his light at Christ's crucifixion: And as the darkness which was spread over Egypt was followed by the destruction of their first born, and of Pharaoh and his host; so the darkness of Christ's death was the forerunner of the destruction of the Jews. Moses foretold the calamities which would befall the nation for their disobedience; so did Christ. The spirit which was in Moses was conferred in some degree upon the seventy elders, and they prophesied; Christ conferred miraculous powers upon his seventy disciples. Moses was victorious over powerful kings and great nations; so was Christ by the effects of his religion, and by the fall of those who persecuted his church. Moses conquered Amalek by holding up both his hands; Christ overcame his and our enemies when his hands were fastened to the cross. Moses interceded for transgressors, and caused an atonement to be made for them, and stopped the wrath of God; so did Christ. Moses ratified a covenant between God and the people by sprinkling them with blood; Christ with his own blood. Moses desired to die for the people, and prayed that God would forgive them, or blot him out of his book; Christ did more, he died for sinners. Moses instituted the Passover, when a lamb was sacrificed, none of whose bones were to be broken, and whose blood protected the people from destruction: Christ was that paschal lamb. Moses lifted up the serpent, that they who looked upon him might be healed of their mortal wounds; Christ was that serpent. All Moses's affection towards the people, all his cares and toils on their account were repaid by them with ingratitude, murmuring, and rebellion; the same returns the Jews made to Christ for all his benefits. Moses was ill used by his own family, his brother and sister rebelled against him; there was a time when Christ's own brethren believed not in him. Moses had a very wicked and perverse generation committed to his care and conduct, and to enable him to rule them, miraculous powers were given to him, and he used his utmost endeavor to make the people obedient to God, and to save them from ruin; but in vain; in the space of forty years they all fell in the wilderness except two: Christ also was given to a generation not less wicked and perverse, his instructions and his miracles were lost upon them, and in about the same space of time, after they had rejected him, they were destroyed. Moses was very meek above all men that were on the face of the earth; so was

Christ. The people could not enter into the land of promise till Moses was dead; by the death of Christ the kingdom of heaven was opened to believers. In the death of Moses and Christ there is also a resemblance of some circumstances: Moses died, in one sense, for the iniquities of the people; it was their rebellion which was the occasion for it, which drew down the displeasure of God upon them and upon him; Moses went up in the sight of the people, to the top of mount Nebo, and there he died, when he was in perfect vigor, when 'his eye was not dim, nor his natural force abated.' Christ suffered for the sins of men, and was led up, in the presence of the people, to mount Calvary, where he died in the flower of his age, and when he was in his full natural strength. Neither Moses nor Christ, as far as we may collect from sacred history, were ever sick, or felt any bodily decay or infirmity, which would have rendered them unfit for the toils they underwent; their sufferings were of another kind. Moses was buried, and no man knew where his body lay; nor could the Jews find the body of Christ. Lastly, as Moses a little before his death promised 'another prophet;' so Christ 'another comforter.'

"The great similitude consists in their both being lawgivers, which no prophet ever was besides Moses and Christ. They may resemble each other in several other features, and a fruitful imagination may find out a likeness where there is none. But as the same excellent writer concludes, 'Is this similitude and correspondence in so many things between Moses and Christ the effect of mere chance? Let us search all the records of universal history, and see if we can find a man who was so like to Moses as Christ was, and so like to Christ as Moses was. If we cannot find such a one, then have we found him of whom Moses in the law, and the prophets did write, Jesus of Nazareth, the Son of God.'

"III. There is no want of many words to prove, for it is visible to all the world, that the people have been and still are severely punished for their infidelity and disobedience to this prophet. The prophecy is clear and express; 'Unto him ye shall hearken: And it shall come to pass that whosoever will not hearken unto my words which he shall speak in my name, I will require it of him,' that is, I will severely punish him for it, as the phrase signifies elsewhere. The antecedent is put for the consequent: judges first inquired, then punished; and the Seventy translate it, 'I will take vengeance of him.' This prophecy, as we have proved at large, evidently relates to Jesus Christ. God himself in a manner applies it to him: for when he was transfigured, Matt. 17:5, there came 'a voice out of the clouds, which said, This is my beloved Son, in whom I am well pleased: hear ye him;' alluding plainly to the words of Moses, 'Unto him ye shall hearken,' and so pointing him out for the prophet like unto Moses. St. Peter, as we noted before, directly applies it to our Savior, Acts 3:22-23,—'For Moses truly said unto the fathers, A prophet shall the Lord your God raise up unto you, of your brethren, like unto me, him shall ye hear in all things whatsoever he shall say unto you: And it shall come to pass, that every soul which will not hear that prophet, shall be destroyed from among the people;' which is the sense rather than the words of the prophecy. And hath not this terrible denunciation been fully executed upon the Jews? Was not the complete excision of that incredulous nation, soon after Jesus had finished his ministry among them, and his apostles had likewise preached in vain, the fulfilling of the threat upon them for not hearkening unto him? We may be the more certain of this application, as our Savior himself not only denounced the same destruction, but also foretold the signs, the manner, and the circumstances of it, with a particularity and exactness that will amaze us, as we shall see in a proper place: and those of the Jews who believed in his name, by remembering the caution and following the advice which he had given them, escaped from the general ruin of their country, like firebrands plucked out of the fire. The main body of the nation either perished in their infidelity, or were carried captive into all nations: and have they not ever since persisted in the same infidelity, been obnoxious to the same punishment, and been a vagabond, distressed, and miserable people in the earth? The hand of God was scarce ever more visible in any of his dispensations. We must be blind not to see it: and seeing, we cannot but admire, and adore it. What other probable account can they themselves give of their long captivity, dispersion, and misery. Their former captivity for the punishment of all their wickedness and idolatry lasted only seventy years: but they have lived in their present dispersion, even though they have been no idolaters, now these seventeen hundred years, and yet without any immediate prospect of their restoration: and what enormous crime could have drawn down, and unrepented of still continues to draw down, these heavy judgments upon them? We say that they were cut off for their infidelity; and that when they shall turn to the faith, they will be grafted in again. One would think it should be worth their while to try the experiment. Sure we are, that they have long been monuments of God's justice; we believe, that upon their faith and repentance they will become again objects of his mercy; and in the meantime with St. Paul, Rom 10:1—'Our heart's desire and prayer to God for Israel is, that they may be saved.'"[1]

H. L. HASTINGS' LIST OF LIKENESSES

The following points of similarity between Moses and Christ may somewhat indicate to the candid reader the truthfulness of the prediction of the great Lawgiver, that a prophet like unto him shall arise:

1. Moses was born of poor parents, under the reign of Pharaoh,

---

[1] Thomas Newton, Dissertations on the Prophecies, 14th Edition. London: Isaac & Hinton, 1829, pp. 84-89.

a cruel and oppressive tyrant: like him, Christ was born in poverty, and under the reign of Herod, a cruel oppressor.

2. Moses was persecuted in infancy, and doomed to die by Pharaoh; Christ was also persecuted in infancy, by Herod who sought the young child's life.

3. Moses was wonderfully preserved in Egypt by providential interposition, while other infants were destroyed; like him, Christ, by providential interposition, escaped the wrath of Herod, by whose command the infants of Bethlehem were slain.

4 Moses, notwithstanding all his wisdom and learning spent years of his life toiling as a humble laborer, a shepherd in the wilderness of Midian, before he was manifested as a deliverer of Israel: like him, Christ, though at twelve years old the doctors were astonished at his wisdom, was yet subject to his parents, and toiled till manhood as a carpenter in Nazareth.

5. Moses went forth from the wilderness, and was revealed to Israel by mighty signs and wonders which he wrought: in like manner, Christ emerged from the carpenter's shop in Nazareth, and, by the miracles he did, demonstrated his divine authority.

6. Moses fasted forty days upon the mountain top in the wilderness of Sinai, communing with God; like him, Christ fasted forty days in the wilderness of Judea, tempted by Satan and ministered to by angels.

7. Moses had the offer of high dignity as the son of Pharaoh's daughter, but refused the proffered honor, choosing rather to suffer affliction with the people of God, than to enjoy the pleasures of sin for a season: like him, Christ spurned the offer of all the kingdoms of the world, and the glory of them, and condescended to be a man of sorrows and acquainted with grief, despised and rejected of men.

8. Moses was faithful as a servant, obeying all the commands of God: like him, Christ, not as a servant but as a son, was faithful

over his house, it being his meat and drink to do the will of his Father that sent him.

9. Moses delivered his people from the bondage of Egypt: like him, Christ came to deliver men from the bondage of sin and corruption, to proclaim the opening of prison-doors, to break every yoke, and to set the captives free.

10. By his wonder-working power Moses had control over the very elements, and divided the sea whose waves' roared: like him, Christ was able to rebuke the winds and the waves, saying, 'Peace, be still; and there was a great calm.'

11. Moses was the founder of a State, the first republic the world ever knew; like him Christ was the founder of a vast community of equal brethren, which has since spread into all parts of the world.

12. Moses, unlike other prophets, was permitted to talk with God face to face upon the mountain: like him, Christ had personal communion with the Father, as no other prophet ever had.

13. Moses had such fellowship with God upon the mount that his face shone with glory, and required to be veiled: like him, Christ prayed on a mountain until he was transfigured in the presence of his disciples, and his raiment was white as the light, and his face did shine like the sun.

14. Moses foretold the future history of the people of Israel, and of the world, and his predictions have been accomplished, and are known to be true: like him, Christ foretold the future destiny of his church in the world, and of the Jewish people, and the predictions which he uttered have been fulfilled, and are being fulfilled today.

15. Moses led Israel through the desert, while manna was showered from heaven to satisfy their wants; like him, Christ repeatedly fed thousands who were faint and hungry in the wilderness, and he still gives the living bread, the bread of God, to satisfy

his hungry people.

16. Moses smote the rock and brought forth water for the children of Israel who were dying with thirst; like him, Christ bestows the living water, being himself the smitten rock, the Rock of ages, cleft for the salvation of a lost world; and he cries in the ears of a dying race, 'If any man thirst, let him come unto me and drink!'

17. Moses was the mediator of a covenant made between God and man, a covenant sealed with blood, and bestowing inestimable blessings upon the people: like him, Christ was the mediator of a new and better covenant, a covenant sealed with more precious blood, and conferring still greater benefits and blessings on those who enter into agreement with their Maker.

18. Moses was very meek, above all the men upon the earth; bearing Israel's provocations and faults with patient affection and tender love, but the meekness and tenderness of Christ was still greater, and his long-suffering was more abundant.

19. The Israelites murmured and rebelled against Moses, who was their best and truest friend: and this also was true of Christ for 'they hated him without a cause.'

20. Moses lived to benefit his nation, and finally died on account of their sins: like him, Christ spent his life in lowly service, and then bore the sins of men 'in his own body on the tree' so that 'with his stripes' they might be healed.

21. Moses was buried by the hand of God in an unknown grave, and seems to have been raised up from death by Michael the archangel, since he appeared upon the mount of transfiguration in glory, with Elijah who had never died: like him, Christ died and was buried and raised again, and entered into the glory, and sits at God s right hand till he shall come to judge the world.

22. Moses' greatest works were accomplished after his death, his law leaving its impress on the world for more than thirty centuries, and marking him as the most influential man that ever lived:

like him, Christ's real work only commenced when his earthly career was finished, and in its ever-widening influence through eighteen hundred years, shows him to be the Son of God, the Savior of the world, the mightiest being who ever wore the human form.

23. Of Moses it is said, 'There arose not a prophet since in Israel like unto Moses, whom the Lord knew face to face in all the signs and the wonders which the Lord sent him to do.' (Deut. 34:10-12). Like him, Christ was 'a prophet mighty in deed and word before God and all the people' (Luke 24:19), 'approved of God among you by miracles and wonders and signs, which God did by him' (Acts 2:22), doing among them 'the works which none other man did.' (John 15:24).

24. Finally, Moses was the first and only man whom the Lord ever authorized to give laws to Israel; the law given by Moses being the only authoritative rule bestowed by God for the government of that nation. In like manner, Christ is the last and only person whom God has authorized to give laws for the government of mankind, the 'one lawgiver, who is able to save and to destroy.' And though the law given by Moses has been corrupted by the traditions of the elders, and the truth revealed in Christ has been perverted and distorted by his professed servants, yet both Moses and Christ still stand forth in unapproached and unapproachable excellence, as revealers of the divine will to the sons of men [Christ, of course, spoke through the men whom He inspired by the Spirit, J.D.B.]

Here, then, is the prophecy by Moses of the coming of a Prophet like himself: and for more than 1450 years the Jewish nation read and studied it, and pronounced it yet unfulfilled. No man had arisen in Israel like unto Moses, during all this time. And had the skeptic of today lived there, this would doubtless have been set down as one of the 'Mistakes of Moses,' a prophecy uttered which had never been fulfilled.

When Christ came, the question arose again and again, as he wrought his wonders, 'Art thou that Prophet?' In him, at last, it was seen that this prediction was fulfilled. We may search all the records of universal history, and we cannot find a man who was so much like Moses as was Christ, not a man who was so much like Christ as was Moses. And hence we are led to conclude, as we read the record of the life of Jesus, the prophet of Galilee, that we have found 'Him of whom Moses in the law and the prophets did write,' the promised Messiah. Let those men who make themselves merry over the 'Mistakes of Moses,' lead such a life as Moses did, and leave behind them a record of a prophecy such as he uttered, and then, through the perspective of future ages, it will be easy for later generations to determine whether they have spoken wisely when discussing the 'Mistakes of Moses,' or whether they themselves have not been more grievously mistake in their course.

Moses spoke of the Savior and the Lawgiver that was to come, and the Lord declared, 'It shall come to pass that whosoever will not hearken unto my words which he shall speak in my name, I will require it of him.' (Deut. 18:19). 'Him shall ye hear in all things, whatsoever he shall say unto you. And it shall come to pass that every soul which will not hear that prophet, shall be destroyed from among the people.' (Acts 3:22, 23). The 'Mistakes of Moses' may be a theme for careless merriment, and the amusement of an idle hour, but he who refuses to hear that prophet whom Moses foretold, may find in the Great Day of accounts, that he has made a greater mistake, and one which it is beyond his power to rectify.

May that Law which came by Moses, be our guide to bring us to Jesus the true Messiah, whose gospel is 'the power of God unto Salvation, to the Jew first and also to the Greek.'[2]

---

[2] H. L. Hastings, Remarks on the Mistakes of Moses, Boston, Mass: Scrip-

tural Tract Depository, 1893, pp 27-31.

A Line of Prophets?

Some maintain that the prophet like unto Moses was not one special prophet, but the line of prophets who came after Moses to teach and lead the people. In commenting on Deut. 18:15-18, Joseph Reider, a Jewish author, said: "Our passage, according to Ibn Ezra, has particular reference to Joshua, the successor of Moses. Others think the allusion is not to one prophet, but to a succession of prophets, arising whenever the need arises for ascertaining the will of God."[1]

It is argued that the term is collective because in Deut. 18:20-22, although the prophet is singular, each and every false prophet is included in this denunciation. The context, however, shows that it is speaking of any prophet who would do this thing and characterizes the one that should die as one who is "such a prophet."

God sent prophets to Israel from time to time. "Since the day that your fathers came forth out of the land of Egypt unto this day, I have sent unto you all my servants the prophets, daily rising up early and sending them..." (Jer. 7:25). This series of prophets culminated in the sending of His own Son. This is true, but in the light of the passage itself as well as other passages in the Old Testament, we do not think that this is its meaning.

In Christendom there have been those who have agreed that this prophecy must be divested of its Messianic application; but, as J.M. Hirschfelder points out, they "differ among themselves in applying it. Some find its fulfillment in Joshua, and some in Isaiah,

---

[1] Joseph Reider, **Deuteronomy,** Philadelphia: The Jewish Publication Society of America, 1948, p. 180.

others in Jeremiah, and others again in a line of prophets. One surely has a right to expect, when critics are so ready to controvert a deeply rooted and generally received opinion, they would at least be prepared to propose something substantial in its place but here, it will be perceived, we have nothing more but mere conjecture on their part, in fact, critic arrayed against critic."[2]

After arguing that the prophecy referred to an individual, Christ, Hengstenberg maintained that the prophetic office, and thus other prophets, was included. "But how can these two facts be reconciled:—that Moses had undeniably, the Messiah in view, and that, notwithstanding, there seems at the same time to be a reference to the prophets in general? The simplest mode of reconciling them is the following. The prophet here is an *ideal* person, comprehending all the true prophets who had appeared from Moses to Christ, including the latter. But Moses does not here speak of the prophets as a collective body, to which, at the close, Christ also belonged, as it were, incidentally, and as one among the many, as *Calvin* and other interpreters mentioned above suppose; but rather, the plurality of the prophets is, for this reason only, comprehended by Moses in an *ideal* unity, that, on the authority of Gen. 49:10, and by the illumination of the Holy Spirit, he knew that the prophetical order would, at some future time, centre in a real person, in Christ. But there is so much the more of truth in thus viewing the prophet order as a whole since according to 1 Pet. 1:11, the Spirit of Christ spoke in the prophets. Thus, in a certain sense, Christ is the only prophet."[3] "Thus there is a concurrent reference to the other prophets, not in their individual capacities, but only in relation to the Spirit, who though in a manner not yet completed,

---

[2] **J.M.** Hirschfelder, "Messianic Prophecy", **The Canadian Methodist Quarterly,** Vol. Ill, p. 225.

[3] E. W. Hengstenberg, **Christology of the Old Testament,** Vol. I, p. 115.

was powerfully efficient in them, and conjoined them along with their Head in one united body. They were viewed *in Christ,* as they were but his instruments: his Spirit constituted the essence of their office."[4]

Hengstenberg argued for this wider application—to a line of prophets—on the following grounds. *First,* the wider context demanded it. Deuteronomy had spoken of judges and officers (Deut. 16:18), priests and Levites (17:9), of a king (17:14) of the priests (Deut. 18:1-8), and had warned them against false teachers (18:9-14). Therefore, it would be natural for God also to make reference to the institution of the prophets. However, this does not follow. The presence of prophets is implied in the tests that they were given to detect false prophets (Deut. 13:1-5; 18:20-22). But the prophets were not an institution or order such as the magistrates and priests for whose selection specific requirements were given. Priests, for example, came from the tribe of Levi. However, the prophets were not selected as were the priests. God raised up prophets when and where He saw fit, and out of whatever tribe He wanted to select. Although sometimes we find a reference to the schools of the prophets, yet the prophets did not make up an order as did priests and magistrates. Furthermore, there is nothing in Deuteronomy which says that God was instituting an order of prophets in Deut. 18:15-18 as He instituted magistrates, or priests.

Second, Hengstenberg felt that if Deut. 18:15-18 does not include the prophetic office, and a line of prophets, the prophetic office was without any legitimate authority.[5] However, one does not have to find the prophetic office in these verses in order to learn from many other verses that God did send prophets from time to time to Israel, and that they were legitimate because God sent

---

[4] As quoted by John Pye Smith, **The Scripture Testimony to the Messiah**, London: Jackson and Walford, 1837, Vol. I, p. 252.

[5] *Op. **Cit.,*** p. 114.

them. And God did not say that He sent them on the grounds that the prophetic office was instituted in Deut. 18:15-18.

Charles A. Briggs argued that there is insufficient authority for viewing "prophet" as a collective. "The Samaritans base their Messianic hope on this passage, rejecting all later prophecy, and interpret it as referring to a Messianic prophet. The context is also in favor of an individual prophet; for the prophet is not only represented as coming forth from Israel, but is also compared with Moses, and thus presumptively he is an individual likewise. It is true that the Mosaic instruction makes no provision for an order of prophets. But it is not necessary that it should so do. Later prophecy does not depend on the Pentateuch for its authority, but upon God Himself, who called the prophets immediately and sent them forth as He did Moses. The reign of Jahveh [Jehovah, J.D.B.] the King of Israel, was immediate and continuous over His people. The priest code prescribed an order of priests, but nothing further. Jahveh, the theocratic King, reigned over the people, and He commissioned whom He would to speak and act for Him; and herein was the guarantee for the perpetuity and unfolding of divine revelation. It was necessary that the priestly organization of the people should be always complete; for their communion with their God must be continuous and unbroken. But it was not necessary that there should be an unbroken and continuous unfolding of divine revelation. God made new revelations of His will as the people were trained by the older revelation to receive them; so that in some cases development was rapid, in other cases tardy. It was not even necessary that the royal organization of the people should be always complete and unbroken. The princes of the tribes as the representatives of Jahveh communed with their King through the *Urim and Thummim;* only on critical occasions was a princely mediator required, and he was always called forth by Jahveh when needed. The divine Spirit came upon such men as Joshua and Gideon, and they led the people and delivered them from their ene-mies. The prophetic ministry was fulfilled as a rule through the in-structions, written or unwritten, in the hands of the people. It was only when these needed unfolding that Jahveh summoned a proph-et to reveal His will, to increase and enlarge the material of the di-vine revelation. And hence no official prophet appeared in Israel until Samuel, the last of the judges and the father of a new era. The prophetic office of Moses was not transmitted to his successors. And hence there was nothing in the historical or psychological ex-perience of Moses to incline him to predict an order of prophets. The very fact of the distinction between his own ministry and that of the Levitical priesthood in this particular would incline him to look for one summoned directly by Jahveh like himself, without predecessors or successors. Thus, in accordance with the general principle of prophecy, he sees the Messianic end in which the di-vine instruction left incomplete by himself will be completed by a prophet greater than himself; but he does not see all the intervening steps to that end. He sees only that first stadium in which false prophets and magicians appear to mislead the people."[6]

Third, Hengstenberg argued that the immediate context de-manded a wider interpretation than just to Jesus. Moses had for-bidden access to the diviners, etc., of paganism (Deut. 18:9-14), and also gave them a way in which to test false prophets (Deut. 18:20-22). Hengstenberg implies that it was but natural that in be-tween these statements would come the assurance that although they were not to consult pagan wizards, or follow false prophets, they would not be left without true prophets of God. This would all be very well if Moses had said, in Deut. 18:15-19, that God would not leave them without true prophets; but this is not what Moses said. Instead, as has already been pointed out, Moses referred to a

---

[6] "Messianic Prophecy," pp. 112-113.

prophet like unto him, and the other prophets were not like unto Moses. Of course, the prophet like unto Moses would have to pass the test of successful signs; for if he did not he would be a false prophet whom they should reject—as Moses taught (Deut. 18:20-22). Moses himself, but not these authors today, put the prophecy in such a way that it does not fit into a context of ordinary prophets. Although it may seem strange to some that Moses did it this way, this is the way that Moses did it. Israel was not left helpless, even if there was no prophet at a particular time, for Israel had the law, teachers and priests.

PROPHETS AS TYPES

There are others who maintain that although the word "prophet" is to be taken collectively here and means a line of prophetic teachers, the Messiah is included in this series as the pre-eminent one in whom the promise culminates. Thus S.R. Driver in the *International Critical Commentary,* which does not accept the passage as a direct prophecy of the Messiah, said: "The terms of the description are such that it may be reasonably understood as including a reference to the ideal prophet, Who should be 'like' Moses in a pre-eminent degree, in Whom the line of individual prophets should culminate, and Who should exhibit the characteristics of the prophet in their fullest perfection." Joseph Klausner, a Jewish author, thought that the roots of the messianic idea are to be found in the figure and work of Moses.[7] Whether this be the case or not, it indicates that some Jewish scholars recognize there is a likeness, in some sense, between Moses and the Messiah which goes beyond any similarity between Moses and the other prophets.

One does not repudiate the fact of prediction just because he

---

[7] Joseph Klausner, *Op. Cit.,* pp. 14-18. Millar Burrows, review of Klausner's *The Messianic Idea in Israel,* in the *Journal of Biblical Literature,* p. 150.

may think that this prophecy refers to a line of prophets which culminates in, and is perfectly accomplished in, Christ. Those who deny the fact of divine prediction refer it to a line of prophets, but some affirm the fact of prediction but maintain that a line of prophets is meant. Calvin, for example, upheld the reality of direct predictions of the Messiah, but he thought that in this passage other prophets were included.

William J. Beecher maintained that "Scholars are correct in saying that the word 'prophet' is not here a collective, but denotes one prophet and no more. All the same, however, the word is here used distributively. The prophets will be a succession, and each one will have the typical character. As the word 'Messiah' denotes the successive kings of the line of David, with the possibility that the line may culminate in a greater King, so there is a possibility that the line of prophets may culminate in a greater Prophet."[8] However, if each prophet as a prophet typified Christ, it was certain, and not just a possibility, that the line of prophets would culminate in Him whom each prophet typified.

It should be kept in mind that both Jews and Christians recognize that the prophets spoke in a variety of manners. This is affirmed in the New Testament (Heb. 1:1-2), and by such Jewish authors as Joseph Klausner, in his book on Messianic prophecy, who point out that some of the prophets spoke in the language of the types. Thus David, who was a type of Christ, was used in such Messianic prophecies as Ezekiel 37:24-26. A type was an Old Testament individual, institution or event which bore some point of resemblance to something or someone in connection with the Messianic age. A prophet, therefore, could be a type of Christ the great prophet. Thus one could maintain that the line of prophets, thought

---

[8] William J. Beecher, **The Prophets and the Promise,** Grand Rapids, Michigan: Baker Book House, 1963, p. 351.

of as a series of individual prophets, could typify Christ the great prophet. Moses could have spoken of individual prophets who would each as a prophet be a type of Christ as a prophet. Since, however, the one who was typified was greater than the one who typified him—as Christ is greater than David who typified Him—Just so Christ the prophet is greater than those prophets who typified Him.

In such a case each prophet would be, as John Pye Smith points out, "no more than an imperfect accomplishment of the promise. The likeness to Moses required to be filled up: the statement being made so pointedly in the singular number, both the times, is not rationally accounted for, on the interpretation that a number and succession were alone intended: and the great guiding principle of the prophetic system, a constant convergence to the Messiah and his kingdom, eminently warrants, or rather demands the other, as the *ultimate and principle design*"[9]

As Seiler suggested, "If this passage speaks of all the prophets of God, can it have failed to speak of Him who is *the greatest of them all?* And which of the prophets was more like to Moses than Jesus was? Moses was the lawgiver and the teacher of his people; and such was Christ, but in a far more exalted and excellent manner. Moses was, under God's wise direction, the founder of the best system of religion that his age admitted of: the same and much more was Jesus the Founder of the supremely best religion that men are capable of receiving. Moses delivered the Israelites from Egyptian servitude and temporal death, by the blood of the Paschal lamb: Christ hath delivered us from eternal death by the shedding of His own blood, and from the slavery of sin by the operation of the Holy Spirit through the truth. Moses was the general and leader of his nation; as the chieftain of the Israelitish community, he ad-

---

[9] Smith, *The Scripture Testimony* to the Messiah, Vol. I, p. 248.

ministered their affairs, and led them in the wilderness: Christ is the Sovereign and Head of his church, he leads us through the wilderness of this life, he protects us from our enemies, he governs us by the truths of his gospel. When Israel sinned, Moses more than once obtained by his supplications forgiveness for them from God; but he could only deliver his countrymen from temporal punishments. Jesus Christ is the Intercessor at the right hand of God: on the cross he obtained the forgiveness of our sins; he is our Representative, and the Author to us of the everlasting salvation. Moses only declared the manna which God gave from the skies and directed the Israelites to gather it: Christ could say, 'I am the Bread of Life, which cometh down from heaven; he that eateth of me shall live forever.' Moses could lead the Israelites no further than to the borders of Canaan, and there, unable to enter that goodly land, he died: Christ leads us into the celestial Canaan, and will there forever satiate us with the fruits of faith and holiness. He is the 'Prophet like unto Moses;' but far, yea infinitely greater than Moses,"[10]

If Moses meant that he, and each of the prophets who would follow, typified Christ, then it would follow—as on the other interpretation also—that Christ would complete the revelation given through Moses and fulfill it. For the type typified something to come which would fulfill the type, and bring the system of types to an end. The type was superior to the thing which typified it, and thus Christ was superior to Moses. He fulfilled both the law and the prophets (Matt. 5:17-18). He brought them to an end in that He was the consummation toward which they looked, which they promised, and for which they prepared.

---

[10] As quoted in Smith, *op. cit.*, Vol. I, p. 251.

ONE PROPHET MEANT

Concerning the use of the Hebrew term, prophet, in this place, Hirschfelder wrote that it did not apply to a collective. "We maintain that such an application of the Hebrew term is altogether inadmissible, inasmuch as it is never used *collectively* throughout the Old Testament, but has always the *plural form* when denoting prophets. The only attempt that has been made to show the *collective* use of the term is by a reference to Daniel 9:24, but the word *nabbi* is evidently there used in the sense of "prophecy, as it stands in connection with "vision" and is so rendered both in the Authorized and Revised Versions. What sense would it make to render 'and to seal up the vision and the prophets?' Many Hebrew words are used sometimes in a wider sense, as (erets), *land* or *country,* for its *inhabitants;* (adamah), *ground* or *earth,* for its *produce;* and so (nabbi), *prophet,* in the above passage in Daniel, for *prophecy."* [11]

If Daniel 9:24 does use the singular, "prophet," for the collective, "prophets," it would be an unusual exception which was demanded by the context. However, there is nothing in the context of Deut. 18:15-18, or elsewhere, which shows that we should interpret "prophet" as "prophets." Dr. William F. Beck, who thought Dan. 9:24 was an exception, said: "In Hebrew 'sheep' in singular often means a flock of sheep, and 'the Canaanite' regularly means the Canaanites. Such singular nouns used for groups we call collectives. But with one exception in Dan. 9:24 'prophet' isn't used as collective. Like the word, 'priest,' of which we have the regular plural in Deut. 18:1, 3, the plural 'prophets' was used for more than one. Our text speaks of 'a prophet' and 'him' as an individual." [12]

---

[11] *Ibid.,* p. 224.

[12] Dr. William F. Beck, "Like Moses", **The Lutheran News,** November 28, 1966, p. **7.**

William H. Thomson argues that the collective interpretation is contrary to the context. "This whole interpretation, however, is open to the obvious criticism that nothing can make it appear as the natural sense of the wording of the passage in question. The exposition that the words 'a prophet—like unto me—unto him shall ye hearken—my words in his mouth,' etc., are so impersonal and general that they mean all the prophets of after-times, suggests a strain to the rules of grammar which savors too much of theoretical exigencies to account for it. There is no parallel in the Hebrew of the Bible, or indeed in any other language, to the employment of a singular noun with singular suffixes as a collective or generic term in the fashion in which the phrase 'a prophet' is used, both directly and by reference, throughout this passage.

"The employment of nouns in the singular as generic or collective terms is common to all languages, as in the phrase 'the king can do no wrong;' but the context never fails to show that no particular individual can be meant. A good example of this is to be found, in this very connection, in the latter part of chapter 17, where certain regulations are laid down to be observed by the Nation's King, when such should be chosen. As there can be only one king at a time, these injunctions are legitimately referred to one individual, just as it is usual now to speak of the Pope as if he were always one and the same. But such individual designation would plainly be inadmissible in the case of the numerous contemporary priests and prophets. Thus it is said that even among the mediaeval rabbis, who had every motive to refer these words to another than the Messiah, many of them felt obliged, by the evident construction of the sentences, to choose Joshua or David or Jeremiah as the person meant by the Oracle.

"On the contrary, it may be asked why this unusual and misleading method of designating the prophetic office should have been chosen, when it was not thought of in the parallel case of the order of priests. The latter was not only a more continuous and more organized body than that of the prophets, and therefore more suitable to be spoken of collectively, but also it was distinctly embodied, as it were, in the person of the high priest. Such a sentence, therefore as 'Jehovah will raise unto thee a Priest' might be made to appear, with such effort, as a poetical reference to him who stood as the personification of the priesthood. As no such language or conception in regard to him is to be found, it seems still more unnatural to find it used in reference to an order which never had an official head or representative.

"Without the interference of preconceived ideas, the inference naturally left on the mind by the perusal of this passage is that the nation, by this language, was designedly led to look for the coming of another prophet, who also would be another lawgiver and the sole leader of the people, and in his relation both to God and to them would be the counterpart of him who stood as their mediator on the dread day of Horeb. That this language did have that effect in after-times is well known to have been the case. (John 6:14)."[13]

If ordinary prophets had been meant, it would have been sufficient to say that God would raise up a prophet. God gave His word to the prophets and they gave it to the people. In this respect Moses was not unique, for receiving and delivering the word of God to the people was something which he shared in common with all prophets. But Moses was different, and this difference must consist in something other than the fact that he delivered God's word to the people. That the coming prophet was unique is indicated in the fact that he was to be like Moses. If one speaks of a scientist like unto Einstein he is speaking not of a line of scientists but of a particular scientist. This argument is not primarily based on the fact

---

[13] **William** H. **Thomson,** *The Great **Argument, or Jesus Christ in the Old Testament,*** New York: Harper and Brothers, 1884, pp. 141-142.

that the prophet is individualized but on the fact that "the prophet in question is particularized; he was to be 'a prophet like unto Moses.' Such a resemblance can only be predicted of Jesus of Nazareth, who, like Moses, was the founder of a new dispensation of religion, a legislator as well as a prophet, and (though in a much higher sense) a mediator between God and man."[14]

THE OTHER PROPHETS WERE NOT LIKE MOSES

"The prophet is moreover contrasted with a single individual—with Moses; and this compels us to refer the prophecy to some distinguished individual." For Moses did not say that God will raise up a prophet inferior to me; instead he emphasized that the prophet would be like unto him. There were other teachers sent from God, but Moses was in a class by himself. The Old Testament itself draws a distinction between Moses and the other prophets.[15] Miriam and Aaron once spoke against Moses because of his marriage to the Cushite woman. 'And they said, Hath Jehovah indeed spoken only with Moses? hath he not spoken also with us?' (Num. 12:1, 2). Jehovah told them: "Hear now my words: if there be a prophet among you, I Jehovah will make myself known unto him in a vision, I will speak with him in a dream. My servant Moses is not so; he is faithful in all my house: with him will I speak mouth to mouth, even manifestly, and not in dark speeches; and the form of Jehovah shall he behold: wherefore then were ye not afraid to speak against my servant, against Moses?" (Num. 12:6-8). There would be other prophets, but God did not compare them to Moses. God conversed in a more intimate way with Moses than He did

---

[14] Gloag, *Messianic Prophecies*, p. 137. As quoted by Edward Hartley Dewart, *Jesus the Messiah,* Toronto: William Briggs, 1891, p. 104.

[15] A.B. Davidson, *Old Testament Prophecy,* Edinburgh: T. and T. Clark, 1905, p. 73.

with the other prophets, Moses saw the likeness of the Lord in a way that was not permitted to them. Under the Old Testament, Moses was in a class by himself. The ordinary prophets, and we may thus say the prophetic order, were not like Moses. "Moses, as a prophet, is here contrasted with the whole order of prophets of ordinary gifts."[16]

A KING

The strongest argument which I have seen, that a line of prophets is meant, is made by Gurdon C. Oxtoby who wrote: "The use of the word 'prophet' in the singular, to designate an indefinite number of individuals in succession, is exactly parallel to the phrase in the preceding chapter (Deut. 17:14-15)," where a king does not mean one particular king but the office of kingship.[17] However, we do not believe it to be parallel. *First,* the desire for a king was to come from their own volition, although God would appoint the king (17:14-15). The sending of the prophet was to be entirely of God's volition. However, this is not the most important point in showing that these two cases are not parallel. *Second,* it was indicated that the king would have descendants. The king was to observe the law "to the end that he may prolong his days in his kingdom, he and his children, in the midst of Israel." (17:20). Nothing indicates descendants of the prophet. *Third,* the statement about the king did not say, A king like unto so and so, but only that they wanted a king like the nations around them have. In other words, Israel did not have a king, but the people would want a king because other nations around them had kings. So it is clear that they are speaking of the office of the king and not just one particu-

---

[16] Hengstenberg, *op. cit.*, p. 110, 111.

[17] Gurdon C. Oxtoby, *Prediction and Fulfillment in the Bible,* Philadelphia: The Westminster Press, 1966, p. 108.

lar king. If later God had said He would raise up a king like David, we would expect some particular king who would more nearly resemble David than any other of the kings of Israel. Of the prophet, God did not say that I shall raise up a prophet. He said that He would raise up a prophet of a particular characteristic, i.e., a *prophet like unto Moses* (Deut. 18:15, 18). This leads us to expect not a line of prophets who were unlike Moses, but a prophet who would be unique just as Moses was unique. Deuteronomy expressly denies that prophets who followed Moses were the prophet like unto Moses (34:9-12). If reference were made to a line of prophets, surely Joshua would have been one of them; but neither he nor others were the prophet like unto Moses.

Although we do not deny that there are some things which can be said for the interpretation that it referred to a line of prophets which culminated in Christ, we believe that the weight of the evidence shows that one prophet—the Messiah—is meant.